CW01637816

n

Soul

ELIZABETH FILLEUL

Elizabeth Filleul was born in the West Midlands in 1962 and studied English at Aberystwyth University before training as a journalist with the Birmingham Post and Mail. *Since then, she has worked as press officer of the Sports Council, as editor of* Woman Alive *magazine and as a freelance journalist, writing extensively about eating disorders, sport and fitness and women's issues. In 1990, she travelled solo around the USA, Australasia and Asia, and ended up meeting and – five years later – marrying an Aussie. The couple now live in Melbourne, where Elizabeth works as a book editor for the travel guide publisher, Lonely Planet. In her spare time she enjoys bushwalking, attending sports events and reading crime novels.*

Consuming Passion

Why Diets Harm Body and Soul

ELIZABETH FILLEUL

TRIANGLE

First published in 1996

Triangle
Society for Promoting Christian Knowledge
Marylebone Road
London NW1 4DU

Copyright © Elizabeth Filleul 1996

All rights reserved. No part of this book may be reproduced or transmitted in any form or by any means, electronic or mechanical, including photocopying, recording, or by any information storage and retrieval system, without permission in writing from the publisher.

British Library Cataloguing-in-Publication Data
A catalogue record for this book is available from the British Library

ISBN 0-281-04844-4

Typeset by Pioneer Associates, Perthshire
Printed in Great Britain by
Biddles Ltd, Guildford and Kings Lynn

Contents

Acknowledgements

I would like to thank everyone who helped directly or indirectly in the writing of this book: my parents in whose home I wrote it; the dieters, failed dieters, anorexics, bulimics and compulsive eaters who shared their stories with me; Maureen Morris of Anorexia and Bulimia Care for putting me in touch with eating-disordered Christians; Alice Mahon MP for information on her private member's bill and details of some of the worst excesses of the diet industry; and Naomi Starkey, commissioning editor of Triangle, for her advice and encouragement – and for suggesting the idea to me in the first place.

All Bible quotations are taken from the New Revised Standard Version of the Bible © 1989; they are taken out of context (the Bible does not cover eating disorders!) but I hope they help to illustrate the points being made.

Foreword

We can't live without it. Food: we spend hours every day thinking about it, buying it, preparing it, and clearing up after it. God could have chosen other, less enjoyable ways to sustain our bodies: perhaps by osmosis, or by swallowing, three times a day, a little pill containing exactly the right amount of nutrients. Some of us may wish that he had. Eating, instead of being a source of pleasure, has become a source of intense pain and misery for many people. Few of us are completely immune from the effects of eating problems, whether upon ourselves or others, yet we are so blinkered that they may take us completely by surprise.

'You knew your grandmother suffered from anorexia, of course,' said my grandmother's GP, moments after her death. We were shocked. The idea had never occurred to us, though she had died a wizened little figure, weighing barely more than five and a half stones. We assumed her death was due to a lifetime of cigarette smoking, rather than to a lifetime of starvation. But when we thought about it, it was an obvious explanation for all kinds of behaviour which had puzzled us for years. The way she cooked and baked for hours for her family, but would never sit down and eat a meal with them, even on important Jewish festivals. The way my grandfather ate alone off a tray every day. The way she would almost force food down my throat, taking it as a personal insult if I refused: 'I've stood and made it especially for you', then berate me for putting on too much weight. 'You're far too plump,' she used to say,'the boys won't like you if you're plump.' Plump! What a hateful word. It sounded like lump and made me feel like one. Whereas she, she pointed out, had a tiny waist, and was intensely desirable to men. The truth was she had no breasts, her hair was thin, her skin sagged, her teeth disintegrated, she found it hard to become pregnant, and suffered increasingly from osteoporosis.

I wouldn't want anyone to suffer as she must have done throughout her life. That's why I'm so glad Liz Filleul has tackled what has become a major social disease: worrying about our weight. Three generations of women in my family were blighted by it. My teenage years were misery because my mother, who was on a permanent diet, made me feel that no one would ever like, let alone love me, because of my curves and bulges. I was determined that a fourth generation, my fourteen-year-old daughter, would not be faced with that kind of pressure. I watched every word I said, encouraged her to love food and her body, but didn't reckon on the power of the magazines she reads, the advertising she sees, the false images of ideal womanhood that are thrust at her every day. She complains constantly that her legs, arms, her figure in general, are too flabby. Why? Because of a witless media that tells her that her lithe figure just isn't slim enough.

This book is a must for anyone who is concerned about the damage caused by our obsession with dieting. It made me realise how deceived I had been, how abused society is. It made me angry enough to want to do something about it, to protect my daughter, and my son too, from the kind of exploitation that makes them ashamed to be who and what they are.

We have just returned from a three-week family holiday in a rented house. There were eight of us. Three of the women brought their diets with them. One was high fibre, one was all pulses and nuts, and one was protein only. We ended up shopping and cooking separately. We rarely ate together. Relationships were severely strained. Any chance of communal life was destroyed. It is no coincidence that the most important symbols of the Christian faith are taken orally. A meal is at the very heart of community. At its best it is an act of fellowship. What was intended to build human beings up and draw them together has become a weapon to destroy them and force them apart.

Liz Filleul passionately believes it is time to fight back. Here is hope for all who have a struggle with food, and for those who want to help them. There are practical, positive suggestions for compulsive eaters, dieters and food phobics, and for the churches who so often, albeit unwittingly, compound the problem, rather than bringing wholeness into the situation. There are few such books around. Many will thank God for it.

Michele Guinness

Introduction

When I was ten, I spent my time devouring Enid Blyton's books, listening to records by the Sweet and Donny Osmond, watching *The Adventures of Black Beauty* on television and wishing I had a pony of my own. I told people that when I grew up I wanted to write books like Enid Blyton and be a top international showjumper like Ann Moore. Boys were mates, my favourite meal was steak and kidney pie with chips, and I did not know or care how much I weighed.

That was in 1972. Less than half a century later, thousands of little girls throughout the Western world are counting calories and worrying about their weight, wishing they looked like their Barbie dolls or the stars of *Baywatch.* A 1995 survey revealed that eighty per cent of ten-year-old girls in the USA claimed to be on a diet, while in the United Kingdom, girls as young as seven are being treated for the 'slimmer's disease' anorexia nervosa.

Something is clearly wrong – and it is this disturbing trend towards increasingly younger girls making themselves ill through dieting which prompted British MP Alice Mahon to attempt to introduce strict new laws regulating the £1-billion-a-year slimming industry. At the time of writing, her private member's bill has not yet been passed – but the publicity around it has highlighted major areas of concern.

These include media images which imply that women have to be thin to be beautiful and that men need a firm, muscular body to be attractive. They include the fact that the numerous diets and diet products launched every year do not work in the long term (would there be a need for almost monthly new ones if just one of them did?) and that many of them are detrimental to health.

Hopefully, Ms Mahon's bill will one day be passed and diet manufacturers made more responsible for the often wild claims they make. But it is not just up to Parliament to alter the idea that only thin is beautiful. It is up to all of us.

It is up to us to reject media images which tell us we are failures if our bodies are not a certain shape. It is up to us to accept our bodies and take care of them properly, instead of following 'miracle diets' which, in the end, only make us *gain* weight. It is up to us to affirm others for who they are rather than for the way they look. It is up to parents to ensure that children are as aware of the dangers of dieting as they are of the dangers of alcohol and drugs.

At present, the idea that a beautiful body is a slim, well-toned body has been bought by the whole of Western society, regardless of sex, age, race or culture. In theory, Christians should be the first to accept their own God-given bodies, to care for them and value them. In practice though, most Christians are as concerned about their body image as anybody else – there are even Christian diet books and fitness tapes on the market claiming that Jesus will help you lose weight! Does God *really* appreciate watching millions of Westerners virtually starving their bodies for fashion reasons, while millions in the Third World are starving through famine? Somehow, I think not.

This book is an anti-diet, pro self-acceptance and pro-health. It is aimed at everyone who worries about their weight and body shape and at everyone who is concerned about the harmful effects of dieting, both physical and psychological.

Most importantly, it is aimed at everyone who does not want the current generation of babies to be tomorrow's pre-teen dieters, anorexics and bulimics. Let us all learn to love and care for our God-given, unique bodies and encourage our families, our friends, and our children to value and care for theirs.

1 Anorexia and Bulimia: Going to Extremes

For no one ever hates his own body, but he nourishes and tenderly cares for it, just as Christ does for the church.

Ephesians 5.29

For years, Katie hated her body.

'I started dieting as a teenager,' she recalls. 'I wasn't pretty and I didn't have a great personality. I was clever at school, but other than that I had nothing going for me. In my year at school there were a couple of girls around whom everyone gravitated – they were both short and fragile-looking, no more than about six stone. I was quite short, so I thought if I looked cute and waiflike people would notice me and I would be popular too.'

By following an 800-calories-a-day diet, Katie attained and maintained her desired 'waiflike' frame until her early twenties. Then, her self-control cracked and she found herself bingeing. 'I just couldn't stop eating,' she remembers. 'In front of other people, I would eat nothing or very little. But once I was alone, I would binge on anything – chocolate, biscuits, cake, cereal and especially bread – whole loaves of it. I would even eat frozen bread straight from the freezer – several slices at a time. I was totally out of control, like an addict. I used to take laxatives to get rid of the food and sometimes I would make myself sick. But I was gorging so much, they had no real effect. I gained about three stones in weight over two years.'

As Katie's weight increased, so did her self-hatred. 'By

this time I was working and was not very good at my job. So now, in addition to feeling unattractive and lacking in personality, I also felt useless at work. All I'd had going for me was the fact I could keep myself thin by dieting – and now I could not even do that any more!' She despised herself so much that she began to want to hurt her body. 'I'd lie in bed and fantasize about setting fire to my hair. I would scratch myself hard, leaving scars. Once, on my way to the local park, I scraped my hand along every wall I passed until it was bleeding copiously.'

Katie never sought medical help for her problem. 'I was,' she explains, 'too ashamed of what I was doing to tell my GP. Instead, I read every book I could find on the subject of eating disorders, and tried to follow their advice.' That advice included eating three meals each day, banishing the notion of 'forbidden foods' and learning to listen to her body. Because of her eating habits, she had lost touch with natural feelings of hunger and fullness. A regular churchgoer, Katie also prayed daily about her eating problems. 'I know other people prayed for me too, and those prayers have been answered. It was hard work getting back in touch with my body's real needs – it took about six years before I was truly free of my eating problems. But I was fortunate – some people never recover.'

Katie suffered from bulimia nervosa (see panel at the end of this chapter), an eating disorder which was first named by a British doctor, Gerald Russell, in 1979. It remained a little-known syndrome until 1992, when Andrew Morton's book *Diana: Her True Story*[1] revealed that the Princess of Wales had suffered from bulimia throughout her marriage to Prince Charles. In the wake of these allegations came newspaper and magazine articles on bulimia, TV documentaries on bulimia, and speculation that various other celebrities – including the rock star Elton John – suffered from bulimia.

Until the publication of Morton's book, there had been constant speculation that the weight-conscious Princess Diana suffered from another, better-known eating disorder, anorexia nervosa (see panel). First identified as an emotional disorder in the seventeenth century, anorexia became increasingly widespread throughout the Western world in the 1970s and 1980s. Unlike bulimics, who combine an overwhelming fear of gaining weight with an irresistible urge to eat, sufferers of anorexia eat as little as possible in order to lose weight – and even when they are frighteningly emaciated, cannot be convinced that they do not need to lose a few more pounds.

Christine, now forty-five, is what experts refer to as a 'career anorexic'. She has been on a starvation diet since the age of fifteen. Extremely thin and terrified of gaining weight, Christine's life revolves around her meagre food intake. 'I have a very strict routine, which I find difficult to break. Breakfast is cereal and toast, lunch just an apple, then I have a small supper of more or less the same meal at 8 p.m. every night. During work breaks I *have* to get out for a walk. I would love to be able to sit and relax without feeling agitated, but I can't.' Diagnosed anorexic as a teenager, Christine has received medical treatment for her eating disorder but, to date, nothing has worked. 'I have come to terms with the fact that I must live with the condition and just learn to cope as best I can.'

Despite her pessimism, Christine does try to fight her anorexia. 'I've turned my walks into nature studies to stop myself from thinking about my evening meal. I'm trying to accept more invitations to functions, telling myself it is only one meal away from my routine; it doesn't really matter if I eat later, or don't have my apple to finish the meal.'

According to statistics, there are 200,000 registered anorexics and bulimics in the UK alone at any one time. Because many anorexics and bulimics do not seek medical treatment, the actual figure is far higher. Similarly, while statistics show that one in ten sufferers is male, the embarrassment of admitting to a slimming disease probably prevents many men and boys from seeking help.

The effects of anorexia and bulimia go far beyond an obsession with weight and calories. Personal relationships and social lives are the first things to suffer. The estranged husband of anorexic singer Lena Zavaroni told the press in 1991 that one of the main reasons he left his wife was that they could not enjoy a meal together at home, or with friends. While he tucked into his meal, she would sit in another room, eating nothing. A man I know whose daughter is bulimic once complained that when she binged on peanut butter, jam or chocolate spread, she would eat only from the centre of the jar: 'When you looked in the cupboard, the jar appeared to be full. But when you opened it, it was empty apart from a layer on the sides of the jar.' When empty jars were not replaced in the Saturday morning shopping session because they had appeared to be full, family relations became strained.

Katie recalls that the diet she maintained prior to her bulimia caused a breakdown in her once close relationship with her grandfather. 'I used to visit him one evening a week and we'd have supper together. Then I got that I didn't want to eat it. He would be so hurt that I didn't want his food, that in the end it became easier not to go.'

Social lives often dwindle to nothing for people with eating disorders. Invitations which involve food are turned down. Those that are accepted place the sufferer under pressure: either they sit through the function eating nothing and putting up with other people's comments and wisecracks; or they eat and then worry about weight gain. Melanie, who has been bulimic for two years, remembers overeating at a friend's wedding: 'There was so much lovely food, and once I started eating, I couldn't stop. I lived quite a distance away and on my way home, I stopped at a garage and went into the toilet to vomit up everything I'd eaten. I felt so guilty that the money my friend's parents had spent on my food was being wasted – but the thought of letting it all stay inside was worse.'

For Christian sufferers, this fear of food-based activities can affect their church lives. 'After church services and housegroup meetings you get coffee and biscuits, and there are often buffet-type meals at Christmas or at other times,' says Ginny, an anorexia sufferer. 'People from church invite other members round for a meal or barbecue, which is intimidating if you have an eating disorder. Our church greeted the new pastor with a "welcome tea". It's almost as if church people have no other way of welcoming people and getting to know them. But I guess food events are the norm in all walks of life.'

During the last ten years there has been increased medical research into eating disorders, various self-help and support groups have been established, and various theories have been expounded about the causes of anorexia and bulimia: a fear of growing up, unresolved emotional conflict and lack of self-esteem have all been cited. But none of the increased awareness, help and knowledge has prevented the number of anorexics and bulimics from increasing every year. And these days, even seven-year-olds are being diagnosed anorexic.

While the psychological factors cannot be ignored, there is no doubt that media and social pressures to be thin play a very large part both in causing anorexia and bulimia and in encouraging sufferers to continue to diet. 'The media bombards us with images of beautiful, thin people who are portrayed as very desirable and acceptable,' says Ginny, who regards media pressures to be thin as a major contributory factor in her anorexia. 'Young and impressionable people, and those who are unsure of their own acceptability and desirability are bound to be affected by this. The implication is "I will be happier, more fulfilled and desirable as a person if I am thin and beautiful."'

Heidi, a recovered bulimic, says that while media pressures played little part in the onset of her eating disorder, they had a major role in hindering her recovery. 'Every time I went into a newsagent's or bookshop, there on the shelves would be the latest diet. Most of the women I worked with seemed to be on diets and seemed to spend hours discussing which worked best: Rosemary Conley, Weight Watchers or the F-Plan? I used to want to shriek at them "You're not fat, I'm the one who's fat. And I can't diet because I've got bulimia and can't stop eating!" But, of course, I used to just sit there and say nothing.'

Katie agrees. 'Now I've recovered, I sometimes feel I am the only person who has a healthy attitude towards food. The people I work with – even some of the men – eat for comfort, through boredom or to celebrate something – and then, when they've eaten it, say things like "I shouldn't have had that" and worry about the weight they've put on. They tell me "It's OK for you to eat because you're slim" as if only slim people have the right to enjoy food.'

Katie and Heidi are right – it is not only anorexics and bulimics who worry incessantly about their weight. Millions of people diet and deprive themselves of essential nutrients in their quest to be fashionably slim. Unlike anorexics and bulimics, they would never suspect they had an 'eating problem' – instead they claim to have a 'weight problem' which only increased will-power will solve. They may not fall into the extremes of anorexia and bulimia, but they too are victims of a diet industry which tells them 'slim is in'.

Signs and Symptoms of Anorexia and Bulimia

Anorexia is characterized by rapid weight loss, preoccupation with weight and an obsessional interest in food, calories and cleanliness. Anorexics develop a fear of normal body weight and feel compelled to continue dieting even when they are dangerously thin. They become increasingly withdrawn and socially isolated. They will suffer from constipation, abdominal pains, low blood pressure and extreme sensitivity to cold. Menstrual periods often cease, and hair loss may occur. In extreme cases, teeth fall out and hair appears on the body and face.

Bulimia is harder to detect, because the sufferer is often of average weight or overweight. Bulimics have an insatiable urge to eat combined with an overwhelming fear of putting on weight. They attempt to control their weight by vomiting and/or taking laxatives after bingeing on vast amounts of high-carbohydrate food. They suffer from exhaustion, depression, poor concentration, irritability and social isolation. Bulimics often hide their unhappiness by appearing confident and successful. Physical effects include gum disease, throat infections and possible heart and kidney problems.

2 Feasting and Fasting

He said to his disciples, 'Therefore I tell you, do not worry about your life, what you will eat, or about your body, what you will wear. For life is more than food, and the body more than clothing.'

Luke 12.22–23

Ken is in his early sixties, very trim, extremely fit and has been on a diet for more than forty years. 'It started when I was doing national service,' he explains. 'My nickname then was "Fatty", and I *was* fat as well. I'd been brought up on my mother's cooking – all fried breakfasts and suet puddings. But the army food and exercise helped me to slim down.' Since those days, Ken has avoided fried food, puddings, sweets and anything he considers fattening. Each day he eats a light breakfast, a small evening meal and several pieces of fruit. Occasionally, on holiday, he will splurge on a large breakfast or a pint of beer. He walks several miles each day, and although he lives in the country, he scarcely notices the scenery – for Ken, exercise is the important thing, the sole reason for walking. 'If I ate any more than I do or stopped taking exercise, I would gain weight,' he says confidently. 'If I started having a drink in the evening, or a pudding with my meal, the pounds would pile on within a couple of weeks. I'm happy with my current weight – but it would be nice if I could eat what I liked and remain slim.'

Steve, in his late thirties, is a 'health freak' – he is vegetarian, works out at the gym every night after work, and plays football at weekends. He has recently started a 'liquid diet', which involves replacing breakfast and lunch with fruit drinks and eating an evening meal. His fiancée, Louise, worries about his health: 'He thinks these meal replacement drinks are healthy, but I keep trying to explain to him that he *needs* proper food. At the moment he is very well-toned, but I'm concerned he may become too thin.'

Jane, aged thirty-four, has a similar attitude as Ken towards her weight. She is very slim, eats three healthy meals each day, but only rarely allows herself 'fattening' foods like chips, dessert or a bar of chocolate. 'I like being thin, and would hate to put on weight,' she says. 'I feel terribly guilty if I eat anything I shouldn't.' She plays badminton several times each week to help keep her weight down, and other than that, has no social life at all. 'Counting calories is almost a hobby with me,' she says. 'There's nothing else to do.' Due to careful eating habits acquired in her teens, Jane has never been more than a size eight. But she is far from satisfied with her figure: 'My hips are too big. My ideal figure would be straight up and down, like a ballet dancer.'

Her 34-year-old friend, Marie, envies Jane's will-power and willowy figure. 'I don't know why she worries about her weight, her figure's so perfect. If I were as slim as she is, I would eat whatever I liked.'

Marie's own story is probably typical of millions of yo-yo dieters. 'I started to put on weight when I was about eighteen. Up to then, I had never had a problem. But I was living away from home for the first time and eating too much fast food. When I couldn't get in my clothes, I decided to go on a diet. I had one piece of toast for breakfast, Ryvita and cottage cheese and an apple for lunch, and then something like fish and vegetables or chicken and vegetables in the evening.'

A week into her diet, Marie refused an invitation to go out for a meal with friends. 'I stayed in and watched TV. Then I thought, "It's not fair that they're enjoying themselves and I'm not" so I went down to the local off-licence and bought a can of cider and a large bag of peanuts and a bar of chocolate.' Without realizing it, Marie had begun a feast-and-fast cycle which is still going on.

'I have tried almost every diet – the F-Plan, Rosemary Conley's hip-and-thigh diet, food combining, you name it, I've done it,' says Marie. 'I can keep to it for weeks – then, I'll feel lonely, bored or depressed and will raid the fridge or the biscuit barrel. Then, all the hard work I've put in is ruined in just one night. That makes me feel terrible, so I comfort myself with more food.' Marie claims to feel better when she is on a diet and losing weight. 'I feel more positive if I can fit into size twelve clothes. When I'm bingeing and put on weight, I just feel like a blob.' At the moment she is having what she calls a 'good' phase. 'I'm on a diet, and I play badminton with Jane each week. I know if I lose weight I'll feel attractive again.'

While Ken, Steve and Jane would not be diagnosed anorexic, their attitudes towards weight, food and their bodies are very similar to those of anorexics. Jane may not be emaciated, but she is very, very slim – and she fears weight gain of just two or three pounds would make her fat. Marie is no bulimic; she has never made herself sick or taken laxatives after bingeing. But, like a bulimic, her binges are in secret, she feels out of control around food, and she tries to decrease her weight with ever-more-rigid diets. These people's lives are virtually dominated by worries about weight gain and food intake, but none of them would consider seeking the counselling or medical help they really need.

Irene, who is in her forties, can relate to Marie's problems with food. She, unlike many failed dieters, recognizes that her problem is to do with eating rather than weight. 'My total love of food was there from the beginning,' she says. 'On my way home from school, I always *had* to stop by a sweet shop and buy boxes of Smarties. I just *loved* food. I used to help my mother to bake purely so I could lick the bowls. Years later, I would take butter and sugar in secret, mix them and eat the lot, which is *not* normal behaviour.' Irene, like Marie, has tried virtually every diet and failed to stick to it. 'All diets work,' she says, 'if you stick to them and have control, which is just what the addicted foodie does *not* have. It really annoys me when people say something like "Come on, you can do it" – it's sheer hell when you know you can't.'

For years, Irene tried everything she could to control her eating and lose weight. 'I've had psychotherapy, hypnotherapy and even been to a diet centre and paid to take amphetamines and diuretics. I must have spent thousands of pounds and I'm still six stones overweight.' These days, she recognizes that she has what has been diagnosed by experts as a third eating disorder, compulsive eating. Compulsive eaters are addicted to food in the way that alcoholics are addicted to alcohol. Unlike alcoholics, though, compulsive eaters cannot completely avoid the substance they are addicted to. Everybody has to eat.

'My problems used to start the minute I woke up,' remembers Emma, who started to eat compulsively in her late twenties. 'I used to crave toast. I used to get up and put two pieces of bread in the toaster – but it was never enough. I'd sometimes get through about half a loaf for breakfast, then once I got to work I'd have coffee and biscuits.'

Lunch would be sandwiches and a chocolate bar, and in the afternoon she might eat a cream cake. On the way home, she would eat another bar of chocolate and buy fish and chips, pizza or a Chinese takeaway. 'Because I was working, the last thing I wanted to do in the evening was cook,' she explains. 'I got fatter and fatter and my health really suffered. I seemed to get colds all the time, I had lots of spots, and walking up hills was a joke.'

Occasionally, Emma would summon the will-power to diet and it would last for about a week. 'I used to go on very strict diets – half a grapefruit for breakfast, no lunch, then a Lean Cuisine meal for tea. And I'd go jogging in the local park – I used to feel knackered after a few steps, but would make myself complete a certain distance. I would lose about half a stone in a week. Then I would crack – I'd allow myself a piece of toast for breakfast one morning, and that would be it. Half a loaf later, I was a food addict again, and I would regain the weight I had lost – and usually more.'

Emma found that her social life suffered when she dieted, but it was quite full during periods of bingeing. 'When I was trying to lose weight, I would turn down all invitations involving food. But when I was bingeing, I would look forward to food-centred functions. If I went to the theatre, I would salivate through the first half, thinking about the ice-cream in the interval. Sunday mornings at church were spent thinking about Sunday lunch rather than the sermon.'

Another compulsive eater, Lindy, agrees: 'I enjoy going to church activities where there is food – especially home-made desserts. Sometimes the food is an incentive to go!'

Emma no longer eats compulsively. She began her return to normal eating by identifying foods which 'triggered' a binge. 'Bread, obviously, was something I avoided. Cereal was another. And chocolate was a third. I tried to eat three healthy meals a day, nothing more. I also looked at *why* I overate – it usually happened when I felt bored or lonely, if I'd had a frustrating day at work, when I had lots of energy and nowhere to direct it.'

These days, she eats normally, and can eat two pieces of toast without wanting more. She is totally anti-diet. 'Diets do not work because they don't look at the root of the problem. People who have a problem with overeating should not go on a diet which promises them they will lose a stone in a few weeks by restricting what they eat. They should ask themselves *why* they overeat. It's usually that person's way of coping with stress, and they need to learn new, healthy ways of coping.'

Doreen Williams, a director of the British Christian

organization Anorexia and Bulimia Care (ABC), reported in a recent ABC newsletter that compulsive eating was an increasing problem within the church and that many compulsive eaters were turning to them for help. The fact that so many people who overeat are now recognizing that they have an eating disorder rather than a weight problem is probably due to increased public awareness of the syndrome through the work of such organizations as Diet *b*reakers, Overeaters Anonymous, Anorexia and Bulimia Care and the Eating Disorders Association. Unfortunately, though, for every person who recognizes that dieting is not the answer to their problems, there are thousands who do not – and who continue to try (and fail on) diet after diet, or who, like Jane, maintain a restricted eating pattern which often only makes their lives narrow, obsessional and empty.

In July 1994 the plight of millions of dieters throughout the United Kingdom was voiced in Parliament by the Labour MP for Halifax, Alice Mahon. Horrified to discover that one of her constituents had signed up her ten-year-old daughter with a slimming group, Ms Mahon's worries about the harmful effects of dieting were compounded when she met a teenage anorexic whose menstrual periods had stopped. Ms Mahon's response to these incidents was to try to introduce a private member's bill to regulate the diet industry. She told the House of Commons:

> The Bill that I seek leave to introduce would make provision to regulate the diet industry and to bring weight-loss pills, potions and patches under the Medicines Act. Such a Bill is long overdue. At present, the diet industry can claim virtually anything for its products. When they do not work, the consumer blames herself – for it is usually women who buy such products – and moves on to try the next product.

> Leading health officials in this country, America and Canada agree that dieting is not good for our health. It has been widely established that diets do not work. Ninety-five per cent of dieters regain all the weight loss within two or three years. . . .
>
> Ninety per cent of British women diet at some time during their lives. At any given time fifty per cent of women are dieting, including girls as young as eight and women as old as seventy-five. There is also growing evidence that men and boys are being targeted by the diet industry . . . Dieting undermines women's emotional and physical well-being and is often a step towards serious eating disorders.
>
> The fashion industry and the image makers place enormous pressures on people, and on women and girls in particular, to be unhealthily thin. They imply that unless we can get into a size ten or twelve dress we are no longer attractive . . .
>
> Too many people are suffering at the hands of the pill pedlars and Jack-the-lads selling seaweed patches and other such nonsense. I want to stop it.

Ms Mahon's Bill did not go through Parliament at that reading; it was not successful when she presented it again in February 1995. But, backed by the organization Diet *b*reakers which opposes any diet which is not for medical reasons, she intends to go on pushing for controls on the billion pound diet industry – an industry which is worth six times more than the gross national product of Gambia.

3 *Living off the Fat of the Land: The Diet Industry*

> *Their end is destruction; their god is the belly; and their glory is in their shame; their minds are set on earthly things.*
>
> Philippians 3.19

In my local bookshop, there is an entire section devoted to dieting. There are at least a hundred brightly illustrated, eye-catching titles, Rosemary Conley's *Inch Loss Plan* and *Flat Stomach Plan* prominent amongst them. Other best selling books include Audrey Eyton's *F-Plan Diet* and Judith Wills' *Size 12 in 21 Days*. Clustered around them are other would-be 'diet bibles' such as *The Good Calorie Diet* and *The DIY Diet*. Their authors are less well-known than Rosemary Conley, Audrey Eyton and Judith Wills, but they make the same promise: follow my diet and you *will* lose weight and have the figure you've always wanted.

According to Alice Mahon MP, the promise is a hollow one. Presenting her Bill to regulate the diet industry to the House of Commons in 1994, she asked: 'Why do people like Judith Wills and Rosemary Conley keep producing new books if they have found the perfect solution to weight problems, as they frequently claim? The truth is that they have not found it; like the rest of the diet industry, they are simply out to make money.'

There is certainly a lot of money to be made. Rosemary Conley's *Whole Body Programme*, for instance, grossed £1,417,561 in sales in 1992 alone: it was among that year's fastest selling paperbacks. She has produced several other best selling diet manuals and videos, has her own television slot and compiles special 'New Year, New You' diet plans for tabloid newspapers. Ms Conley discovered her world-famous diet, published as her *Hip and Thigh Diet* by accident in the early 1980s, when she was put on a low-fat diet following a gallstone operation, and lost 'lots of inches' from her hips and thighs.[1] Now a committed Christian, she claims her food plans provide overweight people with 'a healthy way of eating for the rest of their lives' rather than a 'diet', and that thousands of people all over the world have lost weight through her methods. A self-confessed former binge-eater who hated herself when she was overweight, Ms Conley follows her own diet programmes, insists they sell well because they work and regards her manuals as part of her Christian ministry.

While medics and health watchdogs have frequently expressed concern about other best selling diet manuals (such as *The Beverly Hills Diet* and the *NuTron Diet*), Rosemary Conley's eating plans were – generally – initially regarded as healthy. However, there is now some concern that her diets might, in the long term, be harmful to slimmers. Her *Complete Hip and Thigh Diet* – billed as the dieting revolution of the decade – was criticized by the British Heart Foundation: 'The diet consists of avoiding fat completely. In the short term, this does no harm, but a certain amount of fat is needed to enable the absorption of fat soluble vitamins (A, D, E and K) and carotine, and essential fatty acids.'

Whether harmful or not, whether they work or not, Rosemary Conley's books do at least inform the reader that dieting involves effort. Of more widespread concern are those gimmicky diets which appear on the market, promising easy, rapid weight loss. The Advertising Standards Authority states that two out of three claims made for slimming products are bogus – but dieters still fall for them. One of the most notorious 'bogus diets' of recent years was the 'special Chinese tea', Bai Lin, promoted by Peter

Foster, then a boyfriend of former topless model Samantha Fox. Foster used Samantha in an advertising campaign, claiming that she had shed weight by drinking Bai Lin. Following investigations, the tea turned out to be nothing more than a mixture of Typhoo and PG Tips, and, in 1994, Foster was fined £21,000 with £8,000 costs for conning slimmers. But that was after his company, Slimweight, had grossed at least £1.8 million from the tea.

Other slimming cons have included 'anti-fat patches' which turned out to be sticking plasters soaked in seaweed; 'slim as you sleep' tablets which were really capsules containing amino acids and rice flour; and a bogus diet sheet which suggested slimmers ate a whole block of vanilla ice-cream before bed to break down fat reserves.

Gimmicky diets do not come cheaply. A new wonder diet was unleashed in Britain in 1995: 'Thigh and Hip Slim' (nothing to do with Rosemary Conley's *Hip and Thigh Diet*). This diet was apparently developed and clinically tested by US scientists to 'lose those unwanted inches', and warned people 'not to lose weight too quickly'. Wise advice, given the fact that too-rapid weight loss can be dangerous; however, the diet promised women that they could drop from a size eighteen to a size ten dress size in just nine and a half weeks – if that is not quick weight loss, I do not know what is! The fat-busting product was apparently an amino acid and protein complex taken alongside a calorie-controlled nutritional programme. To 'claim your new body – *now!*' would-be-size-tens needed to buy two programmes for every dress size they wanted to drop: four programmes would set them back by £64. Whether it makes any difference to Britain's six million clinically obese people remains to be seen!

A current trend in the diet industry is that towards hypnotic tapes – such as Valerie Austin's *Slim While You Sleep* and Bruce King's *Psycho-Slimming* – which are supposed to help people lose weight (fast) without dieting. In her book *Eating Your Heart Out: Food, Shape and the Body*

Industry,[2] the Australian writer Ramona Koval drew attention to the quasi-religious terminology used by all sections of the diet industry – King's *Psycho-Slimming* is an extreme example of this. Introducing the tape, he says: 'Side one should be played at least once a day . . . to help remind you of the importance of this programme and remind you of the fact that *I am with you all the way*.' (my italics)

Take a look through any diet book, magazine or slimming club literature and the quasi-religious terminology leaps out at you. All diet book authors claim to have discovered 'the "truth"', 'the "only way" to lose weight' or 'a "miracle" solution to weight problems'. There are several slimming magazines available, all of which carry 'success stories' about readers who have managed to shed several stones by dieting. These readers talk about the 'new life' they have discovered since losing weight: 'Losing this weight has made a new woman of me. Not only have I regained my old confidence, but I have gained a new job too'; 'I thought I was fat and happy, until I discovered how good it felt to be slim. And now I know this is the real me, I feel very proud of myself.' At slimming groups, dieters who succeed in losing weight are praised for their 'goodness'; those who cheat are forced to 'confess' that they have indulged in 'sinful' foods. In *Weight Watchers* magazine, slimming group Leaders have a capital L and are spoken of reverently: other slimmers aspire to be Leaders and to 'spread the word' themselves: 'I'm a Leader myself now, and the job is so rewarding. It makes me so happy to see women changing their appearance and feeling so good about themselves. I want to help as many people as I can for as long as possible.'

Success stories are central to slimming magazines: on the covers in large letters and striking colours are captions of the 'I lost two stones – you can too!' variety. Inside, these success stories are always accompanied by 'before' and 'after' photographs of the successful dieter. The 'before' shot is invariably dreadful: an out-of-focus family snapshot of the subject, sporting casual clothes, no make-up and an unkempt hairstyle. The 'after' shot has always been taken by a professional photographer: the subject has had her hair neatly styled, make-up applied by an expert and been given a dress costing over £200 to wear for the occasion. With this treatment, her appearance would still have been greatly enhanced without any weight loss.

And no reader should imagine for one moment that the success stories always represent a happy ending to the dieter's food and weight problems. Weight Watchers' 1991 Success of the Year, Carole Palfreyman, shed more than seven stones, and was rewarded with work-out sessions with the stars and an all-expenses-paid trip to London to buy size twelve clothes. By July 1994, Carole was back up to seventeen stones, and those size twelve clothes she had posed in for the 'I lost weight – you can too' magazine shots hung unused in her wardrobe.

Diet books, slimming magazines, bogus diet products and hypnotic weight-loss tapes are only part of the lucrative diet industry. Slimmers can fork out pounds on video work-outs with well-known actors, sports stars and TV presenters; they can buy home computer programmes which devise diets for all the family. There are ranges of low-calorie snack bars and meal replacements; Weight Watchers – who are owned by the multinational food giant, Heinz – produce a range of low-calorie meals. And those slimmers who lack sufficient 'will-power' to diet alone can join one of the thousands of slimming clubs which offer support and encouragement. For a membership fee, plus a weekly fee (sometimes only payable if the slimmer has failed to lose weight that week), slimmers are given a target weight, a diet sheet, a weekly weigh-in and 'talks' about the benefits of being slim and how to keep within your calorie allowance at Christmas and special occasions.

Sometimes the advice of slimming club leaders can

border on the dubious. One ex-bulimic recalls that her syndrome was sparked off by attending a slimming club: 'The leader advised us to do anything rather than eat – even if it meant sticking a spoon down your throat.' And there is no guarantee that a dieter will achieve long-term weight loss by attending a club. One slimmer, Doris, has attended several slimming clubs and always achieved her target weight: 'The trouble is, once I've reached my weight, I stop going to the group and the pounds start creeping on again.' Her story is typical of many dieters. Some slimming clubs encourage dieters to continue attending meetings once they have reached their target weight – with those who gain weight in any particular week having to pay a fee.

Even more expensive are the slimming clinics, at which qualified doctors can dispense controlled drugs to aid weight loss. In November 1994, the *Bolton Evening News* carried an exclusive report on practises at a diet centre in the north of England, where amphetamine-like tablets were handed out to patients as appetite suppressants. One patient, a mother of three, described to the newspaper how she had suffered a terrifying drugs trip after taking these slimming tablets along with other medication.

According to the newspaper, the woman had registered at the clinic because she wanted to lose a stone. She was given a diet sheet and told to take one Tenuate Dospan tablet per day. The cost of each five-minute session was £10, and it was claimed the slimmer was not told that the tablets were amphetamines. When the weight loss was slow, the dosage was increased to two and a half tablets every day.

The slimmer became anxious and depressed and saw her own GP. She was too embarrassed to mention the other 'prescription' she was taking, and was told to take the antidepressant Prozac. The Tenuate Dospan and Prozac made a lethal cocktail: 'My heart was pounding, my eyes were bulging and bloodshot. I couldn't keep still and kept pacing about. I couldn't breathe properly and I felt like I wanted to jump out of the window,' she told the *Bolton Evening News*.

The British Medical Association (BMA) condemns the use of amphetamine-like drugs for slimming, stating that no one should be given appetite suppressants without good reason – such as having to lose weight for a life-saving operation. The use of such drugs, they say, should be carefully monitored because they are addictive. At the time of the Bolton case, the *British National Formulary* – published jointly by the BMA and the Royal Pharmaceutical Society of Great Britain – also denounced the use of appetite suppressants:

> Use of the amphetamine-like drugs diethylpropion and phentermine is not justified as any possible benefits are outweighed by the risks involved; abuse, particularly of diethylpropion, is an increasing problem.

Open almost any mainstream women's magazine and you will spot advertisements for liposuction and cosmetic surgery. Instead of dieting their fat away, women can now – if they have a few thousand pounds to spare – have it removed with a scalpel. Any imperfections, apparently, can be removed by surgery.

Penny, a 27-year-old woman, has had liposuction to remove fat from her legs. She had always hated her legs, and throughout her teens and twenties wore long skirts and trousers to hide them – even in summer. She was prepared for the financial cost of the operation – but not for the other side-effects. 'If I had known the operation would be so painful, I would not have had it done,' she says. 'I had to take two months off work afterwards, and had to be taught how to walk again. Losing the fat from the backs of my legs affected my balance.'

One woman with no such regrets is Cindy Jackson, who between 1988 and 1994 spent more than £30,000 on cosmetic surgery to improve her looks. Described by the *Daily Mail* as a 'living Cindy doll', the 40-year-old Londoner has had liposuction on her thighs, knees, abdomen and jawline; two nose jobs; facelifts; lines removed from her face; eyes widened and lifted; two chemical peels to her face; and breast implants, which she later had removed. Why? She told the *Daily Mail* that prior to her cosmetic surgery she only attracted ugly and worthless men. So she decided to make herself beautiful, going for what she calls 'conventional Barbie prettiness'. After cosmetic surgery, she says, intelligent, professional and educated men flocked to her side. Yet she told the newspaper that she had no intention of forming a serious relationship with any of those intelligent, professional and educated men: 'I'd marry if I knew the man would never mistreat me, hurt me or leave me, but that's asking for miracles. I don't even want a relationship, which is why I date several men at once. It's all very civilized, lightweight and fun. That's all I want; dates, like Ken and Barbie had.'

When she introduced her proposed Bill to regulate the diet industry, Alice Mahon told the Commons that dieting not only led to serious eating disorders like anorexia and bulimia, but that it led to other health risks, including constipation, headaches, gall stones and depression – all traditionally regarded as 'women's ailments'. She also claimed that dieting brought on mood swings, infertility in some women, and that it caused loss of self-esteem. She argued that all diet products – including books and tapes – should clearly state the risks of rapid weight loss and that permanent weight loss was unlikely and could not be guaranteed. She said that weight-loss centres should display posters on their premises, warning that rapid weight loss might cause serious health problems.

In opposing the Bill, the Conservative MP for Mid-Staffordshire, Michael Fabricant, argued that: 'The only body shapes to which the responsible diet industry encourages women to conform are those that are healthy and comfortable for each individual.' Diet products, he said, were not only safe, but were often extremely successful. And yet he admitted that half the British adult population was overweight, and that the number of women suffering from clinical obesity rose by some fifty per cent during the 1980s – the very decade which spawned numerous best selling diet manuals, including *The F-Plan Diet* and *The Hip and Thigh Diet*.

Feminists have often argued that it is only when 'women's problems' affect men that male-dominated institutions begin to take them seriously. If that is so, maybe it will not be too long before health warnings do appear on diet products – for these days, men and boys are coming under increasing pressure to change their shape. Advertisements of the 'Develop that firm, muscular physique you've always dreamed of . . . *in weeks!*' variety echo the lose-weight ads aimed at women, and frequently appear in tabloid newspapers. More and more men are watching their weight and working out at the gym in response to pressures to be trim and well-toned.

Why is the diet industry so successful? Why do the authors of diet manuals become millionaires? Why do women on low incomes spend money on bogus miracle tea in an attempt to be a stone lighter? Why do women feed mouth-watering meals to their families and eat unappetising meal replacements themselves? What makes a healthy woman like Cindy Jackson spend more than £30,000 on making herself look like a Barbie doll? Why do young men spend money on body-building programmes when most young women find too much muscle ugly?

A 1994 survey of teenagers in Australia revealed part of the answer. The boys who were interviewed claimed that women fancied muscular men. The girls who were interviewed said men fancied pencil-slim women. Yet, when asked what they thought, the girls said too much muscle was a ‘turn-off’ and the boys declared too-skinny women were ‘ugly’.

Their initial opinions of what the opposite sex found attractive were not grounded in reality. Like people of all ages throughout the Western world, their ideas of what others found attractive had been formed by the media.

4 Thin is Beautiful: Media and Fashion Pressures

If with Christ you died to the elemental spirits of the universe, why do you live as if you still belonged to the world? Why do you submit to regulations, 'Do not handle, Do not taste, Do not touch'?

Colossians 2.20–21

For girls growing up in the 1950s, there was only one woman they wanted to look like: her name was Marilyn Monroe, she was the sex symbol of her generation, and she was blonde, beautiful – and a size sixteen.

Today's role models could not be more different from the curvy Marilyn. The women today's girls want to emulate are size six to eight supermodels like Kate Moss, Naomi Campbell and Claudia Schiffer – all extremely thin and extremely rich. Kate Moss, the most emaciated of them all, earns about £7,000 per day.

Until the beginning of 1995, the fashion industry dismissed the idea that super-thin supermodels were partly responsible for the increase in eating disorders among teenage girls. All that changed when an 18-year-old anorexic teenager told newspapers she was dieting because she wanted to look like Kate Moss. Clare O'Sullivan was 5 ft tall and weighed just five stone. Bullied at school and desperately wanting to be popular, Clare scanned teenage magazines for advice. 'All the models were slim,' she said. 'I thought if I looked like them, everyone would like me. Kate Moss looks wonderful. I want to be like her.'

On reading Clare's story, Kate Moss appealed to the

teenager to eat: 'I don't diet. My shape is natural because I exercise. Dieting is very dangerous for you. It ruins your metabolism.' Whether or not Kate's underfed appearance is natural (and some people in the fashion industry have hinted that it is not), her thinness combined with her glamorous lifestyle flash only one message to young girls: look like me and you too can be rich and successful and have a rock star boyfriend.

But it is not Kate Moss's fault that extreme thinness is in vogue. The real fault lies with the fashion industry, which snapped her up at the age of fourteen and turned her into a media icon. When the Clare O'Sullivan story broke, Twiggy, the super-thin model of the 1960s era, defended Kate: 'I got blamed for anorexia, but I always ate well – anything, absolute rubbish. It wasn't my fault that fashion decided to go thin. I just happened to be the one that they picked on.'

But the celebration of thinness does not end with Kate Moss and the other supermodels. It is *everywhere*. Flip through the pages of any mainstream women's magazine, and you will find the following: a diet; cookery pages in which the woman is pictured preparing food or presenting it to her family, but not eating it herself; an interview with a pencil-slim celebrity; a fashion spread featuring thin, young models. And, of course, the woman on the cover is slim, youthful and wrinkle-free. Diets and pictures of young, cellulite-free models are even found within the pages of Christian women's magazines, where the emphasis is supposed to be on inner beauty and 'the whole woman'. Indeed, any magazine which is expected to be read by a high proportion of women is likely to be targeted by the diet industry for weight-loss advertisements – the classified section of *Yours* magazine, which is aimed at retired people, has carried advertisements for 'B-Slim immediately' corsets alongside advertisements for hearing aids, zimmer frames, stairlifts and incontinence pads!

'Easy' diet plans also feature regularly in newspapers – particularly tabloid dailies and Sunday supplements. These diets are particularly prominent in the summer ('Slim into that tiny bikini – *now!*'), in the run-up to Christmas ('Don't be a Christmas pudding!') and at New Year ('Make this year the year you finally shed that excess flab!'). But the diet message does not end there. Tabloid newspapers in particular constantly portray – and describe – slim women as desirable and larger women as 'frumpy'. This was always particularly evident in newspaper columnists' comments about Princess Diana and the Duchess of York, with Diana constantly praised for being slim and Fergie castigated for being an overeating 'Duchess of Pork'. From the minute both women arrived on the Royal scene, the tabloid press seemed obsessed with their weight. Any slight sign of weight gain by Princess Diana was highlighted in photo captions of the 'Diana showed a less-than-trim-tum when she wore her bikini on the beach yesterday' variety, even when it became apparent that she was suffering from some kind of eating disorder. The revelation in 1992 that Princess Diana had been bulimic did not alter the tabloid press's attitude towards unemaciated women one iota.

Television is another culprit. Television advertisements for anything from coffee through to jeans generally feature very slim women and trim, washboard-stomached men. Men and women without an ounce of spare flesh on them advertise low-calorie cereals and low-fat margarine, and the implication is that anyone who uses these products will end up looking like them. Commercials show weight loss as being of primary importance to women: in one ad, a woman decides she would rather have a low-calorie chocolate drink than a date with a good-looking man. Another ad, for the Magnum ice-cream bar, conjures up emotions which women in particular are supposed to feel when eating 'naughty but nice' food: 'I feel guilty,' simpers one, 'I feel reckless,' breathes another. One would have thought there are far more reckless things a woman can do than tuck into an ice-cream bar, but apparently it struck a chord with women throughout the UK, becoming one of the most effective advertisements ever for ice-cream.

Models in advertisements are not only slim, but are also portrayed as having it all: business suit, big house, flashy sportscar, good-looking, caring partner. It reinforces the 'new life' element stressed by the diet industry: lose weight and you will also be rich, successful, popular and lucky in love. Real life may contradict that message – Princess Diana. for example, has not exactly been lucky in love, despite her much-admired figure – but many people still believe it all the same.

Many TV programmes also carry that message – particularly those enjoyed by teenagers. One of the most popular programmes for young people at the moment is the American show *Baywatch*. Whether male or female, all the lifeboat crew are slim and good-looking, and so are the sunbathers on the beach. (Compare that with real beaches, where sunbathers come in all shapes and sizes.) *Baywatch* has made a household name of actress Pamela Anderson, whose hourglass figure, pretty face and golden, flowing locks have made her the envy of millions of teenage girls and the heartthrob of millions of men. Psychologist Martin Lloyd-Elliott, author of the body-language book, *The Secrets of Attraction*, praised Pamela's 'perfect' eyes, mouth, legs and figure, and called her 'the real life identikit woman of most men's dreams'. Identikit is right: according to the tabloids, Pamela Anderson has had breast implants and plastic surgery on her lips, and dyes her hair blonde.

Hollywood is notorious for producing 'perfect, plastic' people, but the fact that film heroes and heroines invariably have superb bodies is bound to make an impression on people in general and insecure teenagers in particular. Irene, who has struggled with compulsive eating and failed diets for twenty years, points out: 'Beautiful, thin people are portrayed as very desirable and acceptable in all areas of the media, and this image is very attractive to a young, impressionable mind or to someone who is unsure of their own desirability or acceptability. Being thin can be seen as an answer to their problems. Even health promotion leaflets use attractive, thin people with well-proportioned bodies, who also look comfortable and well-off.'

Comedienne Dawn French was among the first stars to complain about the lack of non-skinny women on TV. She has launched a range of clothes for plumper women, and has written, produced and acted in a number of successful TV series. But as Katie, who has recovered from bulimia, points out: 'It seems to be only comediennes who provide an "alternative" image to the skinny look. All credit to them – I admire Dawn French for taking a stand, I think she's very talented and funny and extremely pretty. But somehow the fact that she's a comedienne makes me think of the old adage "fat and jolly". Where are the overweight serious actresses or the overweight female sex symbols? Where are the overweight female newsreaders or overweight female presenters? Where, for that matter, are the television presenters who aren't super-thin or overweight, but somewhere in the middle? You still get some paunchy male presenters on TV, but the women are always tiny.'

It is not just female actresses and presenters who apparently have to be thin to be on TV – this extends even to female sports stars. Television has long been criticized by feminists for showing only male sports and ignoring the women's events. The male programme controllers argue that the reason they do not screen women's sports is because no one is interested in them. Yet there is one sport where they show far more coverage of the women's events than the men's: gymnastics. The teenage 'women' gymnastics stars – revered by thousands of young girls throughout the world – are so small and frail-looking that they make models like Kate Moss appear big and clumsy. Additionally, women who reach the top in other sports are as likely to be criticized for their appearance as any other woman celebrity – for example, the ice dancer Jayne Torvill was dismissed as 'fat' by columnists when she competed in the 1994 Winter Olympics. At thirty-six, she was old enough to be the mother of some of her rivals, fit and agile enough to win a bronze medal, and still weighed less than eight stones. But she was heavier than when she had won a gold medal ten years earlier and that was, apparently, a good enough reason for some writers to ridicule her.

Because women in the limelight are criticized constantly by the media if their figures are not pencil-slim, it is not surprising that so many of them end up suffering from eating disorders: Princess Diana is probably the best-known celebrity sufferer, but the American singer Karen Carpenter was – to date – the most tragic. One half of the brother-and-sister duo The Carpenters, Karen died in 1983 of heart failure brought on by anorexia. She was just thirty-two years old. Eleven years before her death, Karen had read a review of a Carpenters concert, which stated: 'Karen may look like the girl next door you'd never peek over the fence at, but she really can sing'.[1] The same article may have praised the Carpenters for producing 'the best-sounding pop show I'd heard anywhere . . . I wouldn't have missed it for the world', but it was lost on Karen Carpenter who never believed that she was pretty enough to be a singing star. She starved herself, swallowed laxatives and emetics and even took thyroid tablets to make her heart beat faster and burn off more calories in her effort to lose weight.[2]

In the wake of Karen Carpenter's death, newspapers and magazines began to publish more articles on the dangers of dieting. Television documentaries and chat shows about anorexia also proliferated. The revelations about Princess Diana's eating disorder in 1992 meant that bulimia too became a household word. And while the Eating Disorders Association claimed that many anorexics and bulimics plucked up the courage to seek help after reading about Diana's problems, both the celebrity sufferers and media coverage of eating disorders came in for criticism. TV's agony aunt Clare Rayner criticized Princess Diana for 'coming out' about her eating disorder – Ms Rayner declared that Diana looked too good on it, and would inadvertently *encourage* young women to vomit up their meals in an attempt to look like her. In a sense, having an eating disorder became fashionable. 'Every other TV personality seems to have had an eating disorder at some time or another,' says Isabel, an anorexic. 'The media makes the illness seem glamorous.' Heidi, a recovered bulimic agrees: 'If I tell anyone I've had bulimia, they become fascinated, and ask me lots of questions about it. They seem more interested in the bulimia than they are in me. And my mother, who was embarrassed by my illness initially, is now almost proud to tell people that I've had the same eating problem as Princess Diana.'

However, an 'anorexia story' broke in 1994 which made eating disorders seem far from glamorous. It concerned anorexic twins, one of whom, Michaela, had died from the illness. The other, Samantha, had dieted down to just four stones and, until she was sent to Canada for treatment, looked as if she too was likely to die from the disorder. Kerry, an 'occasional dieter', says: 'That was the first time I'd ever realised that you *can* be too thin. Those twins looked grotesque.'

Another criticism of media coverage of eating disorders is that some articles and documentaries can teach anorexics and bulimics new tricks. 'I didn't know how to make myself sick until I read an article about a bulimic who induced vomit by drinking vinegar mixed with soapy water, and then stuck a toothbrush down her throat,' says Katie. 'I'm sure there are bulimics around who would never have thought of being sick or taking laxatives after meals if they hadn't read about others doing so.' Katie believes that being thin and on a diet is to the 1990s what smoking was to the 1930s. 'In those days, smoking was seen as a very glamorous thing to do. You see it all the time in old black and white films – smoking looked sophisticated. And these days it's thinness which is presented as being glamorous. That's why so many happy, healthy teenagers start worrying unnecessarily about their weight.'

Rosemary Conley, however, argues, 'We have to accept

that we wouldn't actually buy a women's magazine if an overweight person was on the cover. That is a *fact*.'[3] It is not the media's fault, she says, if women want magazine models to look the way they would really like to be. Women's magazine editors and fashion editors would agree with this, saying that using larger models results in lower sales. The truth of this was borne out in a surprising quarter in 1992, when a Christian publishing company commissioned research into what female churchgoers wanted from a Christian women's magazine. Initially, the interviewees insisted that they did not want to see young, perfect models on the magazine cover: they wanted real women there, warts and all. However, shown a magazine with a picture of a middle-aged, slightly plump, ordinary woman on the cover, several of them exclaimed: 'She's ugly! I wouldn't buy that! She shouldn't be on a magazine cover!' Society, it seems, regards slimness as successful and being overweight as failure just as much as the media does.

Natural Features – Natural Money Market

Women in particular are made to feel guilty and anxious about their weight through both direct and subtle pressure from the media and fashion industry. But they are also made to feel unattractive and insecure about other natural features, such as wrinkles and body hair.

'When I was in my twenties and bulimic, the first thing I used to notice when I looked in the mirror each morning was the size of my stomach,' says Katie. 'Now I'm in my thirties, I don't notice my stomach. Instead, I notice the lines around my eyes. And there seem to be so many ads for anti-wrinkle creams and age-defying make-up. And the models they use are too young to *have* lines around their eyes anyway. But somehow, having these lines can make me feel so *old* and unattractive – as if my youth is over. I'm still single – and, it's stupid, but on days where I feel a bit low, I wonder, will I ever find a man now I've got wrinkles and a handful of grey hairs? It's as if my worries and insecurities about my body have been transferred to my face. Sometimes I think whatever age I am, the media and society will make me hung up about *something*.'

Katie is among millions of women who spend several pounds each month having her legs waxed. 'I used to use creams, but they didn't work too well. The first time I had my legs waxed, it was really painful, but it gets easier the more times you have them done. Having my legs waxed is against everything I believe – as a Christian, I believe we were created by God and should be comfortable with our natural bodies. As a feminist, I don't see why we should get rid of body hair just so we are more attractive to men. The trouble is, like everyone else, I've been conditioned into thinking smooth legs make women cosmetically more attractive – so I have them waxed.'

These days, though, many men feel anxious about such natural things as greying hair, balding and too much body hair. Since the media reported that the tennis star Andre Agassi had had his chest waxed, it became apparent that he was not the only man to visit a waxer – most waxers claim to have at least a couple of male clients. Various treatments for hair regrowth and disguising grey hair appear in tabloid newspapers and men's magazines.

'These days, looks seem to be everything, and men can feel as insecure as women if they feel they are ageing or losing their looks,' says Tom, who is retired and in his early fifties. 'It has been claimed that people who are older or less attractive are less likely to be selected for jobs – I think this is probably more likely to affect women, but it is increasingly bothering men.'

5 Skin Deep: Beauty, Diet and Society

Do you not know that your body is a temple of the Holy Spirit within you, which you have from God, and that you are not your own? For you were bought with a price; therefore glorify God in your body.

1 Corinthians 6.19–20

When Romania's communist dictatorship was toppled in 1989, the plight of the pitiful babies and children in the country's state orphanages was revealed to the world for the first time. Until government legislation halted it, many orphans were bought from parents or smuggled out of Romania to be adopted by Westerners. Among the various controversies this caused was a seemingly small, but telling one: the children the Westerners' hearts went out to most were the cutest and prettiest ones.

In the former Soviet Union, when very young children were selected for specialized training in subjective sports like gymnastics and ice skating, if two showed equal aptitude and there was just one place available, it would be given to the best-looking one. The more attractive the sports star, the more they would appeal to audiences and judges.

Wherever you come from, there is no escaping the importance of being attractive; when you meet someone for the first time, the immediate thing you notice is the way they look. The trouble today is that only certain looks are considered attractive – slimness being paramount among them. Being slim and conventionally good-looking remains of primary importance within society, long past the first impressions stage. Those who do not fall into the category of what is considered attractive can feel marginalized from childhood through to old age. 'I was told I was plain and plump as a child and I still feel unattractive. Those childhood taunts still hurt as much as they ever did,' says Doris, who is in her fifties.

The looks issue begins from the moment a baby is born. If the baby is bonny, there will be a chorus of approving noises from visitors who come to see it. The sight of a less than bonny baby will not precipitate a natural, immediate, admiring reaction. How much this affects the baby as it grows is a moot point – but once it does grow, the psychological and physical advantages of being pretty or cute and the disadvantages of not being either become more apparent.

'I was an ugly child, I can see that from photographs,' says Morag, who is in her late twenties. 'When I was about five or six, I had a friend who was very pretty – blonde curls, blue eyes. She had her parents twisted around her little finger, especially her father. All she had to do to avoid being in trouble was look cute and say "Oh, daddy". It was the same at primary school – she was every teacher's pet and everybody wanted to be her friend, because she was so pretty. I wasn't anybody's pet, and it seemed so unfair to me then – to be ignored just because I wasn't pretty.'

Morag believes that the affirmation pretty girls receive helps them in later years when it comes to relationships with men. 'Pretty girls grow up with so much more confidence. They know that boys will fancy them, and, when they're older, that men will fancy them. They don't have to try to get noticed by men they fancy – men just notice them and instantly want to go out with them.' The fact that men always make a beeline for attractive women was what led Cindy Jackson, the 'living Cindy doll' discussed in an earlier chapter, to spend £30,000 on cosmetic surgery: 'I want beauty, I want perfection and I'm simply not interested in having a face with character. If you want to give a woman power, looks are the greatest asset you can give her.'[1]

Morag is now a teacher and says that Cindy Jackson's view of life is probably correct: good-looking children are generally the most popular. 'In most classes, the most popular boy is the best-looking boy – he's usually good at sport, too. And the most popular girl is usually the prettiest girl. Their looks and subsequent popularity generally give them a self-confidence which less good-looking people, unless they're affirmed at home or for some other reason, don't usually have.'

Being good-looking becomes extremely important in teenage years, when children start to take an interest in the opposite sex. Katie remembers the first time she 'fell in love': 'It was an older boy at school, and I was obsessed with him. I wanted him to notice me, and thought he would only fancy me if I was stunningly good-looking. I used to spend ages putting on make-up and styling my hair, trying to look really good. If a spot appeared on my face I would avoid him, because I thought having spots would bring me down in his estimation.'

It is at this stage that many girls start to worry about their figure – though there are disturbing signs these days that girls are becoming figure-conscious long before their teens. This, perhaps, is hardly surprising – dieting is likely to be discussed frequently in the home, little girls (and boys!) are intrigued by their Barbie doll's amazing figure, and Fuzzyfelt Supermodels is among the games they play with. And plump children – particularly the shy, insecure ones – are likely to be teased at school and given a nickname like 'Fatty' or 'Pudding'. (Indeed any child who is different in any way from the accepted 'norm' – even to the extent of wearing the 'wrong' shoes or having an unfashionable hairstyle – is likely to be teased at school and even bullied.)

Generally, though, it is in the teens when girls start to

become conscious of their weight. In teenage years, food like chocolate, cakes and crisps suddenly becomes 'naughty' – but only for girls. Unappetizing crispbreads thinly spread with cottage cheese replace Big Macs for lunch. Clothes are carefully selected to make the figure look thinner. Girls who spent most of their schooldays forming excuses to avoid games suddenly start working out in aerobics classes or swimming twenty lengths each day to help them lose weight. They flip through magazines to find a fast, effective diet and compete with friends to see who can take in the fewest calories each day.

And calorie conversations continue throughout most women's lives. Diets are discussed on student campuses (where eating disorders among women students are so rife that laxatives are said to be passed around like Smarties), in the workplace, at the youth club, at the hairdresser's, in women's meetings, in the churches. Doreen Williams, a director of the Christian organization Anorexia and Bulimia Care, says that even when she has addressed a church or women's meeting about the prevalence of eating disorders within British churches, the subject of dieting will crop up over coffee. Mention the word 'anorexia' and women will look ruefully down at their own figures and joke that they could do with a bit of that. Few people, it seems, question the idea that slimness is desirable – whatever the cost. In one office where I worked, photographs of a topless Duchess of York in 1992 precipitated this comment from a colleague: 'She doesn't have her sister-in-law's figure, that's for sure.' The fact that it had only recently been revealed that Princess Diana maintained her low weight through compulsive vomiting was apparently immaterial.

Society's obsession with dieting is matched by an obsession with food. Birthdays, weddings, baptisms and anniversaries are celebrated with special cakes. After a funeral, the mourners will gather together for a buffet and a drink. Companies entertain clients with a boozy lunch.

Women meet friends for coffee and cakes. Men – and more liberated women – invite their would-be partner out to dinner. Cinema-goers guzzle a carton of popcorn, then go out for a pizza. Success of any kind is rewarded with a celebratory meal. Few social events do not involve eating – and most major religious celebrations, including Christmas and Easter, Diwali and Passover, are marked by special feasts and food treats. Such celebrations are dreaded by those with eating problems – in 1992, one young female bulimic so dreaded the thought of having to eat a Christmas dinner that she faked her abduction. Her subsequent 'confession' to police was reported in the national press. Both the Eating Disorders Association and Anorexia and Bulimia Care say they receive more pleas for help in the aftermath of Christmas than at any other time.

Despite feminism and the advent of 'new men', the burden of preparing daily meals and sumptuous festive feasts still falls mainly on women. Thus there is pressure on them to provide food – but also to remain slim. As Ramona Koval points out in *Eating Your Heart Out: Food, Shape and the Body Industry*,[2] it has been suggested that to the modern woman, food is like sex was to the women of the Victorian era – women were meant to provide it for their husbands, but were not supposed to enjoy it themselves. Tellingly, in my local bookstore, that vast section on dieting is directly opposite (in both senses of the word) to an even larger section on food, with recipes for baking cakes or cooking with chocolate particularly prominent. And, in an office, if someone buys a round of cream cakes, it will precipitate a guilt trip of the following variety: 'I shouldn't be eating this', 'Never mind, you can diet tomorrow', 'All those calories . . . but cakes are lovely aren't they?', 'Life's not worth living if you can't eat what you like . . .', 'Go on, have one – be a devil . . .' Even the slimmest women join in conversations like this – in fact they are often more bothered than their plumper colleagues by the calorie content of a cake.

Although men and boys are now becoming more figure-conscious, deviations from conventional attractiveness are still tolerated in men far more than in women (apart from in the homosexual community). Men still take part in beer-gut and beer-drinking contests, eating contests and knobbly-knee competitions. None of these would be considered acceptable for women – their equivalents are beauty contests and glamorous granny competitions. Sometimes such competitions act as a barrier to women becoming an accepted part of male-dominated industries. One woman journalist recalls: 'When I became a reporter on a national newspaper, I felt that not only did I have to prove myself by being a *better* journalist than the men, but I had to prove myself by matching them drink for drink after work in the bar.' A young businesswoman remembers her embarrassment at the annual Christmas party when tradition demanded that the last person to join the company had to eat a whole slice of every available dessert. The first woman to be employed at her level of seniority within the company, she struggled through some eight desserts, to 'prove' she was one of the lads – inwardly resenting not only having to eat food she did not want, but also being expected to partake in such a ridiculous ritual in the first place. Emma, a former compulsive eater, gets annoyed at comments made by men when she buys a bar of chocolate from a shop or a cake in a cafe: 'Often a man – usually middle-aged or older – will say "You'll get fat on that." It's meant as a joke, but it's not funny to me – and it wouldn't be funny to an anorexic or bulimic girl. Why do people feel free to say something which can be so very destructive? After all, nobody would say, "You'll get cancer from that" to a stranger who smoked.'

Pretty girls may well grow up feeling more confident about relationships in general and with men in particular, but even the most stunning young women are not immune to feeling insecure and worried about their weight. Nicole started to diet at twenty, and slimmed down from a size twelve to a size eight. Now in her early thirties, she says: 'The whole thing was ridiculous. I'd always been the best-looking girl at school, and was never without a boyfriend and a string of other admirers. But at college, I got hooked on this slimming idea. The consensus was that being very thin was attractive and what men wanted. It wasn't the case – I looked quite haggard when I was a size eight. But while men like women's curves, I do think there's pressure on them to have a stick insect for a girlfriend, because that's the way society says girls should be. I think that men's ideal woman would be one who is pencil-slim with her clothes on but somehow has plenty to grab hold of with them off!'

When Nicole was dieting, her best friend Vicky was verging on anorexia. Vicky recalls: 'I *hated* Nicole for dieting and getting thin. She was so much more beautiful than me – she had *everything* in terms of looks, but she was slightly plump. I was thin, and that was all I had. Whenever we went out together, men fawned all over her and ignored me. I wished she would stay plump so I could be superior to her in something. As her weight dropped, the only thing I could do was lose more weight too.'

Vicky's reaction is indicative of the resentment many women feel towards attractive and slimmer women. As one man noticed, 'At parties men look at the women, and women look at other women.' For women, appearance can be divisive. Blonde women are dismissed by other women as brainless 'bimbos', overweight women are often regarded as 'gluttonous', anorexic or bulimic women as 'stupid'. Katie says that even though she has recovered from bulimia, she still dislikes women who are thinner than she is. 'It's silly, I know, but I can't help it. If I see someone who is thinner, however ugly their thinness may be, I see them as more powerful, more successful, more important than myself.'

In her book, *Fat is a Spiritual Issue*,[3] ex-compulsive eater Jo Ind recalls how she once found it difficult to accept that thin people experienced pain: 'Fiona might have been upset about her boyfriend but she was slim enough to catch another one; Anne might have been feeling guilty and worried about her work but at least she did not need to go on a diet; Julie might have been distressed because she was ill, but, well she was thin.'

Things came to a head for Jo when one of her friends, Liz, told her about the death of her (Liz's) mother: 'I wanted to feel the whole agony with her, but I was inhibited because she was thin. "Stop it, Jo. Stop it," I rebuked myself on reflection. "Was it any consolation to Liz that she was thin? Did Joy's slimness help her when she had a stillborn child? Did Tonia's skinniness prevent her from attempting suicide? . . . Just how many thin women do you have to hold, weep with, live with, suffer with before it breaks through into your obsessively protected heart that even being thin does not take away the deep pains of living?"'

At the extreme end of this belief that thinness is all-important comes American model Christine Alt's reaction to the death of anorexic singer Karen Carpenter: 'I remember looking at Karen Carpenter's picture in *People* and thinking "God, how lucky she was because she died thin." I was very envious. I remember saying "How can I get to that point – being really thin without dying?" That's a sick mind. Karen Carpenter was a skeleton.'[4]

There is clearly something wrong with a society in which some folk believe that only fat people can know real unhappiness, in which a model can envy somebody who died of anorexia at a mere thirty-two years of age. Everybody seems to subscribe to the idea that only slimness is attractive – children, teenagers, young businessmen and women, middle-aged men and women, elderly men and women, even Christian men and women.

Jesus may well have instructed his followers not to worry about their bodies and what they ate. But the majority of Christians today do. Some churches run diet clubs of the 'slim-for-him' variety. A diet book aimed at Christians, *Free To Be Slim*,[5] which claimed that Jesus would tell you how much he wanted you to weigh, became a best seller. During the aerobics boom of the late 1980s, evangelical leader's wife Sue Barnett brought out a keep-fit tape especially for Christians (exercising to well-known Christian worship songs). Rosemary Conley was invited to talk about dieting at the Spring Harvest conference of 1992. Anorexics and bulimics who attend churches with a strong emphasis on fasting admit that 'I'm fasting today' serves as a plausible excuse for avoiding eating. In fact, one American Christian writer, Stormie Omartian, advocated fasting as a good way to lose weight in addition to being of spiritual value. Diets are discussed as much in women's church groups as they are in the office. And according to Anorexia and Bulimia Care, the church has more than its fair share of self-confessed anorexics, bulimics and compulsive eaters.

Why has thinness – especially for women – become so desirable that even members of the church, who are supposed to encourage self-acceptance, try desperately to attain it? Contemporary feminist writing has pinpointed part of the answer.

6 Feminist Perspectives

For people are slaves to whatever masters them.

2 Peter 2.19

It has not always been fashionable for women to be thin. European art down the ages shows women as voluptuous, with large breasts and rounded stomachs. Men found these fuller-figured women desirable: in his painting, *The Kermesse*, the seventeenth-century Flemish artist, Rubens, depicted couples dancing and kissing at a village dance, the men grabbing at the women's ample flesh. As has been noted before, as recently as the 1950s, Marilyn Monroe's size sixteen figure was considered the epitome of beauty. By today's standards, Marilyn Monroe would be regarded as extremely overweight – why have things changed so much?

In *Fat Is a Spiritual Issue*, Jo Ind describes her reaction to a Picasso painting, *Nude Woman in a Red Armchair*:

> The whole picture was a delight in her roundness, the smooth circles of her hips, her breasts, her cheeks, her lips, her arms, her ears, her thighs. There was a softness in her voluptuousness, a delicious sensuality. She was undoubtedly beautiful. She was unfashionable.[1]

Jo compared Picasso's woman with the super-thin women who advertise everything from cars to perfume on television today. As a compulsive eater who hated her size fourteen figure, Jo asked herself how she would feel if a 1950s-style model advertised consumer goods. She realized she would feel a whole lot better. She became aware of something important:

> Women felt inadequate under the cult of Media Woman – 96% thought they should change. Their insecurity was being exploited for commercial gain. People were capitalising on woman's discontent with herself.

Wherever there are insecure, vulnerable people, there are always people ready to exploit them – this is as true of the diet industry as it is of some political systems, certain religions and in too many homes and workplaces throughout the world. Interestingly, the diet industry fed on women's insecurities from the opposite angle in the early part of this century: a 1911 advertisement for a product called 'Sargol', carried in *Cosmopolitan* magazine, promised to put '10, 15, yes 20 pounds of good, solid "stay-there" flesh on your bones'. Another advertisement for Sargol, in a 1936 copy of the *Melbourne Herald*, claims to 'transform ugly hollows into graceful curves'. No doubt those 'seven-stone weaklings' of the early twentieth century were as anxious to be fashionably curvy as today's 'size twelve and over fatties' are to be fashionably slim – and someone, somewhere has always got rich on women's insecurities.

Straight-up-and-down figures first became fashionable in the West in the 1920s. Then curves came back – until the 1960s. Since the 1960s, an ever-thinner look has been in vogue, an ever-thinner look is what women try to aspire to, as ever-younger and ever-more-emaciated models take to the catwalk.

Why women? Why thinness? Susie Orbach was the first feminist writer to suggest an answer. Publishing *Fat Is a Feminist Issue*[2] in 1978, Orbach argued that women who suffered from compulsive eating and anorexia (at that stage, bulimia had not been identified as an eating disorder) were, subconsciously, expressing the difficulties women faced in a male-dominated society. Her book became a best-seller. It prompted *Cosmopolitan* magazine to drop its diet column, but it did not prevent a spiralling number of women from developing eating disorders. Feminist writers who have followed Ms Orbach in trying to help women to accept their bodies and throw away the diet sheets have also failed to prevent a proliferation not only of eating disorders but also of diet manuals.

The reason for this is, I believe, not that feminist writers do not provide helpful answers to women's eating problems – they do – but because, unfortunately, the very label 'feminist' puts many women off reading their work. Many women, wrongly, regard feminists in general as a bunch of radical, bra-burning lesbians and do not wish to be associated with them by reading their books. Christian women face an additional hurdle in that some sections of the church have regarded feminism and women's rights with suspicion – church leaders who believe women should be nothing more than silent child-bearers are unlikely to refer an eating disordered member of their congregation to a book like *Fat Is a Feminist Issue*.

Another barrier between writers like Susie Orbach and the women who might be helped by reading their work is the fact that their writing styles border on the academic, and a lot of women with low self-esteem believe they would not have the ability to understand their books. In contrast, diet manuals are easy to follow; their writing styles appeal to the average *Daily Mail* or *Daily Express* reader. It is interesting that Susie Orbach writes very good and challenging articles for the *Guardian*, where, in a sense, she is preaching to the converted. The *Daily Mail* and *Daily Express* readers are satiated with writers advocating the latest diet – and because more women read the tabloids than the broadsheets, the 'do diet' message is the one which is going to reach their ears. The same goes for women's magazines – *Cosmopolitan* may not have a diet column, but far more women read cheaper magazines like *Woman* and *Woman's Own*, which regularly feature diets.

When the American feminist Naomi Wolf published *The*

Beauty Myth[3] in 1990, she came up against a different barrier. Many dieters – and even some feminists – objected to her anti-diet arguments for one reason only: Ms Wolf was slim and stunningly attractive so what right did she have to write a book telling not-so-stunning women not to worry about their looks and weight?

Women who read *The Beauty Myth* found that her main argument – that the emphasis on near-anorexic slimness was an attempt by men to keep women, literally, in the role of the 'little woman' in response to female advances within society – had a ring of truth about it. The vogue for slimness in the 1920s followed close on the heels of women's suffrage (women over thirty were given the vote in Britain in 1918 and the voting age was brought down to twenty-one, on a par with men, in 1928). The 1960s and 1970s witnessed feminism, the pill and the Sex Discrimination Act; they also saw the advent of six and a half stone Twiggy and an obsession with slimness. Coincidence or not – and Wolf believes it is not – there is no doubt that women who are putting their energies into maintaining a fashionably underfed frame are not able to put so much energy into other areas of their lives, including in the workplace. 'I spent so much time worrying about my weight and what I was going to eat and not eat that I was oblivious to everything around me, and nowhere near as effective at work as I should have been,' says Heidi.

Theorists who oppose feminist conclusions argue that Western women are disillusioned with the equality they have achieved with men, and that their disenchantment is coming out in the form of eating disorders, alcohol and drug problems as well as family breakdown. Feminists retort that this is not the case: women are disillusioned because feminism has not yet gone far enough – women are *still* not regarded (by many men and also many women) as equal with men. Britain may well have had a Sex Discrimination Act since 1975, a woman Prime Minister for eleven years, a woman head of MI5 since 1991 and women priests in the Anglican church since 1992, but there is no doubt that the top jobs in most professions remain the exclusive domain of men. Even in librarianship, a profession which traditionally attracts more female employees, the very top jobs are occupied by men. Legislation affecting everybody is man-made: of 651 British MPs elected at the 1992 General Election, only sixty were women. Of 518 Members of the European Parliament, only one in five are female. Women raise families, go out to work (often in poorly paid jobs) and still do far more than their fair share of household chores, but are rarely given a voice when it comes to making decisions which directly affect them.

Ms Orbach, Ms Wolf and other feminist writers on eating disorders believe that women use food as a symbol of emotions they find difficult to express. Food is used by many women to stifle feelings – both large quantities of food and prolonged semi-starvation annihilate emotional pain. Food – or the lack of it – is used to avoid difficult issues; women concentrate on eating or their diet instead of what is really going on in their lives. Food is used by women for relaxation or comfort, because their traditional role as food-provider has led them to equate food with being cared for. Women use food to alleviate boredom, to fill in time, or as something to do to put off an awkward task or decision. Women use food as a punishment – many bulimics and compulsive eaters admit that if they break their diet, they eat more because they feel they 'deserve' to be fat. Women also use food as a reward for doing something well.

Susie Orbach was the first writer to suggest that many overweight women subconsciously prevented themselves from losing weight because their fat was useful to them. Similarly, people who keep themselves too thin find that their underweight frame serves a purpose in their lives. Other feminist writers have agreed with Ms Orbach's theory, and those with an eating disorder admit there are advantages to being fat or thin.

Fatness or Thinness Provide Protection

Beverley is in her mid-thirties and has recently admitted to having an 'eating problem' rather than a 'weight problem'. 'I've realized my fat is my protection from the outside world – it covers up what I'm really feeling inside. It makes me look OK, with an appetite for life as well as food – but inside, I'm scared of showing the real me to people, especially those who think they know me well, like my family and friends.' Vicky, who once bordered on anorexia before becoming a compulsive eater, says: 'Being thin was my protection from being hurt. I thought that if I looked fragile, people wouldn't say unkind things to me or about me.'

Fat Represents Capability

Katie, who has been both an overweight and an underweight bulimic says: 'I work in public relations, and when I was plumper I felt people looked at me and saw me as capable. When I was thin, I looked more like a child, and people didn't take me so seriously. The men I worked for would think I was cute, and virtually patted me on the head! Being plump meant people treated me differently.'

Fatness or Thinness Provide Distance from Personal and Intimate Relationships

Former compulsive eater Paulette Maisner, who runs the Maisner Centre for Eating Disorders in Brighton, says she has never met anyone who has both an eating disorder *and* a satisfying sex life within a loving relationship.[4] One anorexic teenager says: 'I've always been nervous of intimacy, and being thin gives me an asexual look. Men think I'm cute, but they don't fancy me, so I feel comfortable with them. Anyone who fancied me with my figure (five feet tall and five and a half stone) would have to be a pervert.' Beverley, who is overweight, feels comfortable with her fat for the same reason: 'To the men I work with, I'm one of the lads. They like to talk to me, but it's the slim little blondes they fancy – not me.'

Fat is Rebellion Against the Ideal Shape

'I think that, subconsciously, when I overeat I am saying to society "No, I won't starve myself into those size eight jeans just because you say only tiny women are attractive",' says Ros, an overweight bulimic. 'I want to be liked for who I am, not for what I look like.'

Remaining Fat or Thin Maintains the Status Quo

Many overweight people put off doing things – buying a new suit, learning to swim, joining an evening class, even having a foreign holiday – until they have lost weight. Because they do not lose weight, they never do the things they would like to do. Anorexics and bulimics operate in the same way, promising themselves they will do certain things when they are better.

Feminist eating groups – such as the ones held at the Women's Therapy Centre in London – encourage women to look at *themselves* rather than just their problems with food and weight. They encourage self-acceptance and self-knowledge, and ask them to explore why they need to be fat or thin. Their aim is to shift the importance food and dieting has in women's lives, and encourage them to express themselves in different ways. Once food is no longer their primary focus, eating disordered women are able to look at other issues in their lives which may be causing distress – such as relationships. Feminists, along with experts dealing with eating disorders, agree that problems with food and dieting will only go away if the underlying causes are tackled. The answer to any 'weight problem', they say, is not to go on yet another diet, but to ask yourself why you are overeating or why you need to be thin. The emphasis is on finding and being yourself.

Feminists tend to concentrate on the causes of eating disorders among women, but there is now a growing trend towards men and boys worrying about their shape. It is possible that this is because males are having difficulty adjusting to their new, perhaps hazy, role within society. Although young women are now encouraged to have careers, some men are still brought up to think that they should be the family breadwinner – tradition dies hard! This assumed burden must be hard on men in an age where there is no job security. Men – and women too, of course – facing the prospect of redundancy and long-term unemployment can become depressed and feel worthless, and this in turn can lead to eating problems. Generally too, men have more difficulty expressing emotions than women – this applies especially to British men, who are still expected in most quarters to maintain a 'stiff upper lip' whatever sorrows or traumas come their way.

Jill Welbourne, a leading psychologist who works with anorexics and bulimics, believes the increase of eating disorders in Britain since 1980 is due in part to the economic policies of the Conservative government. 'The underlying theory is that they are encouraging competition and individual success, and actively working against collective values,' she told *Woman Alive* magazine in 1993. Certainly, British society in general does seem uncaring – but has it ever really been any different? Women throughout the ages have been born into a patriarchal society, with very little care and support available (indeed there was nothing available until the setting-up of the welfare state). Added to that, eating disorders have increased throughout the Western world since 1980, including in countries with long-term socialist governments, like Australia and Sweden.

Perhaps what *is* missing today throughout the West is a sense of community. Where once people chatted through problems with their neighbour, they now have to spend £20 an hour on talking to a counsellor. Some psychiatrists claim that the success of TV soap operas like *Coronation Street*, *EastEnders* and *Brookside* is partly due to nostalgia for a community spirit long extinguished. The Christian church – especially the evangelical and charismatic wings of it – with its emphasis on care for the whole church family, is attractive to many, because it offers a real sense of belonging to a community found in very few other institutions.

And yet the church has failed to address the dieting issue or to challenge the notion that only slimness is beautiful. According to Anorexia and Bulimia Care, eating disorders are rife within the church – some 400 Christian anorexics and bulimics are on their computer files at any one time, and apparently compulsive eating is a major but as yet untackled problem.

While very little Christian literature on the subject of eating disorders and diet and body image has been published (perhaps because they are seen as 'women's issues' and therefore, until very recently, unimportant and frivolous), there are some contemporary theologians who have shed light on the problem – by looking at the difficulties facing society in general.

Christian Women and Sex

Rachel is in her early thirties, has a well-paid job and lives on her own. She is a compulsive eater and, while she has some male friends, has never had what she calls a 'proper' boyfriend. She has been out on dates but they have been disastrous for one reason: 'I am *terrified* of any kind of intimacy with men. I hate the way they always want to snog and paw you. The thought of full intercourse is terrifying – I just know I would be totally frigid.' Rachel has never admitted this to anybody, not even her closest friends. 'I tell them I'm a virgin because I'm a Christian and don't believe in sex outside marriage. The people at church think I'm *such* a good Christian, because I don't sleep with my boyfriends and am "saving myself" for the right man. I know the truth though, and so does God.'

Rachel grew up in an evangelical free church and attended a youth group in her teens and early twenties. 'Sex was never discussed – it was something you didn't need to know about until you got married. It was crazy really – this was the late seventies and early eighties, and the church's attitude was Victorian. I developed a hang-up about it, partly because church teaching implied sex was "dirty" and wrong, and partly because my family is very non-tactile. I've never even seen my parents hold hands.'

She is lonely and longs for intimacy. 'I wish I had a husband to come home to – I long to curl up on a man's lap, to feel secure and taken care of. But my relationships will never get that far because I am totally frigid. If I won't let a man snog me, he's not going to hang around very long, is he?' Instead of tackling and challenging her fears, Rachel seeks consolation from food.

As we approach the twenty-first century, sex is still a taboo subject within the church. While many churches and individual Christians are able to teach young people that sex is fun in the context of a committed, loving relationship – and that women have as much right to orgasmic pleasure as men do – there are unfortunately some Christians around who will not discuss the subject with their children or the young people in the church at all. Some youngsters are forbidden to peek at secular sex manuals but are offered no alternative form of instruction. Some teenagers react by, as the self-confessed promiscuous daughter of one Christian couple put it, 'carrying out some practical investigation'. Others, like Rachel, grow up to be afraid of the prospect of sex.

Rachel's case may seem extreme, but the majority of eating disordered Christian women of all ages that I have met agree that sex is a factor in their problems with food. Doris, who is in her fifties and a committed churchgoer, has not had sex with her husband for years. She says she never enjoyed it and that, after she gave birth to her second child, she took to staying up late to avoid being 'pressurized' into sex by her husband. She still prefers to watch late night TV and tuck into cheese sandwiches rather than face the prospect of sex. Of ten women who attended a regional Christian eating disorders support group, eight said they had been sexually abused as children, one said she had had sex as a young teenager and still felt guilty about it, and the other had had no sexual relationship at all and, like Rachel, found the thought of it a total turn-off.

7 Less Food, More Faith: The Church's Reaction

I saw all the deeds that are done under the sun; and see, all is vanity and a chasing after wind.

Ecclesiastes 1.14

The American sociologist and Christian speaker Dr Anthony Campolo admitted in his book *Seven Deadly Sins*[1] that there was one sermon he wished he had never preached. It was on the subject of gluttony. Arriving at a Bible conference in Maryland, he had decided that preachers were too apt to deliver sermons on sins their audiences would have been unlikely to commit. Looking around at the well-padded delegates, he noted that gluttony was a common problem and told them that by overdoing the eating they were sinning before God.

In those days, Dr Campolo equated overweight with lack of will-power, and did not understand that the majority of obese people hate their fatness and suffer emotionally because they cannot control their eating. In his chapter 'Gluttony' in *Seven Deadly Sins*, he apologizes for this and sets out some of the reasons why many people cannot stop eating. It is, he says, an addiction similar to alcoholism, which he believes can only be cured by following a programme along the lines of Alcoholics Anonymous, which has proved so effective in treating alcoholics.

Dr Campolo is one of the very few Christian writers and speakers to mention the problem of obesity and overweight within the church, let alone take the trouble to find out about possible underlying causes and solutions. Until the late 1980s when Christian publications began to carry in-depth articles on anorexia and bulimia, the implication was that eating disorders were a problem outside the church, but not within it. Those who did not know God's love might struggle with eating disorders or other addictions, but 'real, committed Christians' did not. Jo Ind,[2] who struggled with compulsive eating and weight gain during her mid- to late teens, recalls praying: 'Father, help me to be strong in you. You said that the Fruit of the Spirit was self-control. Lord, I acknowledge my weakness; past history has assured me of my total lack of ability to control myself. Please work inside me and be strong in me.' Jo believed that God hated her fat and abhorred self-indulgence. She told herself that every bite of food she took was 'one more wound in the body of Jesus'. When she overate, she got on her knees and repented of her sin.

Diet expert Rosemary Conley agrees with Jo's original point of view: 'Being fat . . . affects your Christianity, because . . . if you really hate yourself and can see yourself overeating and bingeing and being gluttonous, you know you're sinning to the Lord.'[3] While Ms Conley believes that if women who are unhappy with their bodies diet and lose weight, they will like what they see in the mirror and will feel more confident and more able to contribute to society, Jo Ind's battle with compulsive eating led her to a different solution: she accepted that God loved her, regardless of whether she was a compulsive eater. She worked at loving her body as it was, and when she craved food, she tried to work out what she *really* wanted deep down. If she was hungry, she allowed herself to have the very food she wanted right then, even if it was highly calorific. As she got more in touch with her body's natural hunger, she found that her desire to eat compulsively gradually faded away. By not dieting, Jo allowed her body to eat what it wanted when it wanted and to find its natural weight.

Katie agrees with Jo's solution and believes the church

should do more to help people with eating disorders and distorted body images. 'I had been a Christian for several years before I became bulimic. I led Bible studies, attended church twice each Sunday, had long prayer times first thing every morning and last thing every night. There was no way I could have told my pastor or any of the church elders that I stuffed myself with food and then puked it up again or took handfuls of laxatives. They would have said that if I were a real Christian, I wouldn't have this problem.'

Many women who have plucked up courage to tell a church leader that they have an eating disorder have met a response which has only damaged them further. Heidi was told that her bulimia was due to demon possession. 'Various home group leaders and other "top Christians" from my church stood around me, laid their hands on me and shouted to the demon to come out. We were there for ages and nothing happened. I didn't know what to do – I didn't really believe bulimia was caused by demon possession, but if I had said so they would have been convinced that I really *was* demon possessed! In the end, one of the church leaders, a woman, stopped what was happening and told me that, in her opinion, I wasn't demon possessed at all.'

Eating disordered people in some churches have been under pressure to be instantly healed from their problem. One anorexic recalls that: 'Many Christians rushed in to "minister" to me – and added to my feelings of rejection and the sense that I was a hopeless case, even to God, by dropping me when they realized a few prayers and Bible verses weren't going to suffice.' Rachel recalls an incident in her church: 'After the meeting, people with a specific problem were encouraged to go forward for prayer. Two supposedly mature Christians were assigned to pray for me. I told them what my problem was and they prayed to Jesus to heal me, told Satan to come out of me, and then one of them, a man, hugged me and said "You're healed now, Rachel." That night, back at home, I binged again. I wasn't healed, but if I'd said I wasn't they would have told me I didn't have the faith to accept my healing.'

It is interesting to note that the majority of eating disordered Christians react to church leadership – and perhaps other authority figures – in the way that they react to the diet industry. Compulsive eaters try almost every diet that comes on the market, and find they do not lose weight – or, if they do, they regain it. Do they write to the diet manufacturer or the diet book author to complain? They do not. They blame themselves, for not having enough will-power. The diet claims to have helped millions of people, so those who fail are obviously just pathetic. Eating disordered people who seek help within their church are prayed for and are told they are healed – but they are not. Do they write to the church leaders to complain? No. They blame themselves, for not having enough faith.

The nonsense of this becomes obvious when compared with the way people react to other consumer goods or advice which fails to work. If a woman buys a pair of shoes which fall apart within a few weeks, does she blame herself for wearing them too much and not taking proper care of them? Of course not. She returns them to the shop and asks for a refund. If a man has a bad cough and is prescribed antibiotics by his doctor, only for the cough to get worse, does he put up with it, believing it is his own fault that he is no better? Of course not. He visits the doctor again, saying the antibiotics are not working, and hopes to be given more effective treatment. People request refunds for faulty CD players, washing machines, telephones and for food that has gone off – but they will not raise a voice in protest about a diet which fails to work. People will complain loudly (and rightly) if their doctor or hospital provides inappropriate medical treatment, but no Christian will raise a voice to protest to church leadership that despite prayers, words of knowledge and healing hands, they remain unwell.

This is unfortunate, because if more people would

protest loudly about diet products which simply do not work, it would prevent other people from being taken in by them and blaming themselves for failure. If more Christians who have been affected adversely by attempts at help within their church would pluck up courage to say so, it would prevent others from suffering silent guilt trips – and leaders and lay people might think more carefully before announcing that someone has been healed. Tragically, there are a minority of people within the church who – wittingly or unwittingly – exploit people's sense of guilt and lack of self-esteem.

Heidi deeply regrets one incident which occurred at a church she visited, with two Christian counsellors who were helping her to combat bulimia. 'I lived with these counsellors for a while and they used to supervise all my meals, and only gave me a little money to spend each day so I could not buy food to binge on,' she says. 'One Sunday, they took me along to a church where they were speaking about their ministry. I always used to wear black, and Mary, the woman counsellor, lent me one of her dresses – it was bright orange, a really gaudy thing, but I didn't feel I could refuse, because they had been so good to me. At the church, they had me up on the platform, and said "Look at this girl. Just a few weeks ago, she was bulimic. Now, we have prayed for her and helped her to receive God's healing. Just a few weeks ago, she felt so badly about herself that she would wear nothing but black. And now look at her!"

'I wish,' Heidi says, 'that I had had the courage to tell that congregation that Mary had made me wear her hideous orange dress, and that I wasn't healed from bulimia at all – if their total control over my food intake was removed, I would just *stuff* myself. But I didn't. I just stood there on the platform, blushing and simpering, and no doubt some poor eating disordered person in the congregation was torturing herself with the words: "Why doesn't God heal me? What am I doing wrong?"'

Part of Anorexia and Bulimia Care's work involves educating churches about eating disorders, and helping them to understand that problems of this nature are extremely unlikely to go away after one prayer. Psychologist Jill Welbourne,[4] herself a committed Christian, agrees with this: 'I think that a key change of mind can happen instantaneously, and may well happen as a result of being prayed for. But if you have been eating in an anorexic or bulimic way, recovery has to come slowly because you have to learn how to eat normally and unlearn how to eat badly and that can't be "zapped" into you. The Holy Spirit, the whole army of angels, archangels, dominions, powers and thrones can zap you – but you still have to learn how to eat three regular meals a day and accept being a stable, healthy weight. That's the practical bit and it takes time.' Experts agree that this applies equally to compulsive eaters and restricted eaters, both of which are out of touch with natural feelings of hunger and fullness.

In his book *The Shattered Lantern: Rediscovering the Felt Presence of God*,[5] theologian Ronald Rolheiser does not mention eating disorders or dieting and body image once. But his theories about why contemporary society has become unaware of God's presence shed a great deal of light on the West's obsession with thinness – and on why many Christians want to see illness of any description healed instantaneously.

Rolheiser highlights the way discontentment and restlessness within Western society have left no room for people to be aware of God or of their surroundings. It is, he says, an age in which the advent of modern technology has made the workplace a busier, ever more demanding place. People are so busy making it to the top of their career that some have to even make appointments in their diary to spend time with their children. This, he says, leads to physical burnout and addictions (he specifies alcohol and drugs, but food and dieting can be included here). Busyness and the need for efficiency, he says, make people more restless,

less patient and unable to concentrate on anything for very long.

This is borne out by the experiences of eating disordered people and dieters featured in this book. Living in an age of instant faxes, instant television entertainment and instant coffee has made people impatient with things which take time. So they want to lose weight *now* rather than be prepared to make changes in their lives which would, in the long term, alter for good their attitude towards food. Those who pray for people with eating disorders (or any other illness) want them to be healed *now* rather than have to devote time every week for possibly years sitting with, talking to and caring for that person.

Rolheiser points out that although people today are busy, they are also bored. They carry out their monotonous tasks, wondering whether it would make any real difference if they did not turn up for work at all. And (although Rolheiser does not cover unemployment), those without work, of course, are even more bored – and very depressed. Often, an unemployed person's depression has as much to do with the success ethic as it does their financial situation:

'Our lives become consumed with the idea that unless we somehow experience everything, travel everywhere, see everything, and are part of a large number of other people's experience, then our own lives are small and meaningless,' writes Rolheiser.

> We become impatient with every hunger, every ache and every non-consummated area within our lives and we become convinced that unless every pleasure we yearn for is tasted, we will be unhappy. . . . Thus it becomes tragic to be alone; to be unmarried; to be married but not completely fulfilled romantically and sexually; to not be good-looking; or be unhealthy, aged or handicapped. It becomes tragic to be caught up in duties and commitments which limit our freedom, tragic to be poor, tragic to go through life and not be able to taste every pleasure on earth and fulfil every potential inside us.

It becomes tragic not to be as slim as Kate Moss, tragic not to be able to eat our way through a plate of cream cakes and remain thin, tragic that the eating disordered person we prayed for after last night's church service still craves chocolate and hates her body.

Rolheiser believes the lack of awareness of God within society stems partly from our self-absorption (we have no time to seek God and when we do have time, believe we could be doing something more 'useful') and partly from the fact that the church has limited God to the extent where he is no longer 'the full, awesome God of creation'. Too many Christians, he believes, try to define the infinite with their finite minds. God is holy and we should not try to limit him. When we do, he says, it leads people away from God: 'God dies within human life when there is no space within which God can be holy.'

Rolheiser believes that only by approaching God through faith rather than trying to understand him, undergoing his presence rather than trying to figure it out and living in holy fear of God can an individual become truly aware of him. Then their eyes will open wide with child-like wonder both at God and his creation. 'When we see our lives correctly,' says Rolheiser, 'we shall see that all is gift.'

Rolheiser doesn't spell it out, but surely that 'all' includes our bodies.

No More Frumpy Image

Irene is in her forties and is a compulsive eater. She is also a committed Christian, but was brought up in a strict church which told women that it was wrong to wear make-up, to have their hair fashionably styled or to do anything which might attract men's attention. The basis for this was presumably 1 Timothy 2.8–10: 'I desire, then, . . . that the women should dress themselves modestly and decently in suitable clothing, not with their hair braided, or with gold, pearls or expensive clothes, but with good works, as is proper for women who profess reverence for God.' Irene claims that because her church stressed this teaching, 'dowdy and frumpy' became the norm for women in the congregation – and that possibly her own desire to be slim and beautiful was partly a rebellion against such teaching. There are still churches which discourage women from wearing make-up and fashionable clothes – and even get them to cover their heads – but generally female churchgoers have swung the other way: they are as bothered about their appearance as anyone else in Western society. While looking dowdy and frumpy is no true witness to a God who was so colourful and vibrant in creation, there can be no doubt that making oneself unhappy and miserable in the pursuit of slimness is no good witness either.

8 Health, Fitness and Who Should Diet

But as it is, God arranged the members in the body, each of them, as he chose . . . If one member suffers, all suffer with it; if one member is honored, all rejoice together with it.

1 Corinthians 12.18, 26

'Show me a woman who diets for health reasons,' says Mary Evans Young, founder of the anti-diet organization Diet *b*reakers, 'and I'll show you a man who reads *Penthouse* for the editorial.'[1]

She is right. Because of our culture's obsession with thinness, even women who *are* put on a diet for health reasons are thrilled when they subsequently become slimmer and, according to society, more attractive. Rosemary Conley is a prime example of this: forced on to a low-fat diet following a gallstone operation, Rosemary was delighted to see inches disappearing from her hips and thighs. Her best selling books were (partly) inspired by that low-fat diet and she claims that millions of women throughout the world have achieved the same results on it as she did. What should be remembered, though, was that Rosemary was initially put on the low-fat diet for medical reasons. Many of those millions of women who buy her books and try her diet will follow it to be fashionably slim – not because their weight is endangering their health.

Ironically those who do diet for fashion reasons often end up endangering their health, especially if they diet for prolonged periods of time or crash diet only to regain lost weight. These health risks are not only in the physical sense – such as potential osteoporosis, loss of menstrual periods and the other effects discussed in Chapters 1 and 2 – but in a broader sense. Health is defined by the World Health Organization (WHO) as 'a state of complete physical, mental and social well-being and not merely the absence of disease or infirmity'. By that definition, are people who worry constantly about their calorie intake and whose lives revolve around food healthy? No. Are people who sit indoors alone every night, munching their way through 'comforting' crisps and cakes healthy? No. Are people who turn down invitations to social events involving food because they do not want to break their diet healthy? No.

Most people, though, do not think of 'health' in terms of the above definition, but form their own ideas – sometimes very strange ones – about what is healthy. Babies and small children who are plump, for example, tend to be regarded as 'healthy', when actually they may be being overfed and set up for a lifetime's battle with fat and eating disorders. Older generations in particular tend to equate plumpness with health – their 'bouncing babies' were probably just plain fat! – presumably because they were brought up in days of tremendous poverty. Someone who was plump at the beginning of the twentieth century was likely to be wealthy – and much healthier than poorer folk, who generally had too little to eat. This obviously remains the case in the Third World, where only people who are rich are likely to be plump. Apparently, in Papua New Guinea, brides-to-be are given plenty of food and not allowed exercise so that they will be plumper and more attractive to their husbands! This could not be more different from the affluent West, where brides-to-be usually try to lose several pounds so they can squeeze into a fashionably small wedding dress.

Fitness is another thing which has become – wrongly – equated with slimness. At the moment I am trying to build up my fitness levels in readiness for some long treks through the Canadian mountains. But whenever I set out for a lengthy walk or get on the exercise bike, someone is bound to protest: 'But you don't need to lose any weight.' But weight has nothing to do with fitness (muscle weighs more than fat, for one thing); slim people are not necessarily fit and fit people are not necessarily slim. Former cricket star Ian Botham, for example, was always on the tubby side and he was certainly extremely fit, and the same goes for the Australian spin bowling sensation, Shane Warne.

The 1980s saw the beginning not only of the fitness boom, but also of the 'healthy eating' craze, with many people becoming more concerned about what they ate. But nutrition experts persistently fail to agree on what is good and what is bad: one year margarine is better for us than butter; another year, someone finds a possible link between asthma and margarine. One year, we are told to cut out potatoes if we want to lose weight; another year, experts claim Britons do not eat enough fibre. One year, we are told to eat less fat; another year, we are told that a certain amount of fat is essential if we are to remain healthy. One year, we are told to keep an eye on our children's calorie intake; another year, we are told that thousands of children are suffering from malnutrition because there are not enough essential minerals and vitamins in their diet.

Small wonder that people are confused about what they should and should not eat. And despite all the literature available on healthy eating, thousands of people still eat an extremely fatty diet and remain overweight (just as all the diets in the world do not seem to have helped the number of Britons who are clinically obese). Incidentally, very few young anorexic and bulimic women take any interest in the nutritional value of what they eat, other than its calorie content.

People (both men and women) who are seriously overweight *do* endanger their health: overweight can lead to heart disease, diabetes and certain cancers. Seriously overweight people can also suffer physical discomforts like shortness of breath, the inability to walk very far, and, if they develop something like arthritis, being too heavy will make the condition less easy to cope with. Doctors who believe that a patient's weight is putting their health at risk will usually advise them to diet and can refer them to a dietician. If patients wish to remain healthy or prevent their condition growing worse, they would obviously be foolish not to follow medical advice. My father, for example, is diabetic and has to follow a special diet, which he sticks to – even though, initially it was hard for him to give up his favourite chocolates and fish and chips! But he realizes that by maintaining the diet, he is prolonging his life.

Some people, though, still find it difficult to diet even when they are told their excess weight is threatening their life. People who cannot diet even in these circumstances are usually those who depend on food to fulfil emotional, not actual, hunger. They crave food like the alcoholic craves alcohol – and crave it even more when something happens to worry and upset them. Being told that their weight is jeopardizing their health can actually make their food addiction worse – because they know of no other way to deal with their fears and worries. Anyone who falls into this category would benefit greatly from attending a compulsive eating self-help group or by undergoing counselling for food addiction in addition to trying to follow medical advice. By finding out why food is so important to them and finding other, more positive ways of expressing their feelings, they would find that – in the long term – eating became less of an issue, and that any necessary weight loss was easier.

Similarly, people who are told to *gain* weight for health reasons and find themselves reluctant to do so because they like being too thin, would also benefit from attending a support group or receiving one-to-one counselling.

The 1990s, which so far have seen more and more

people admit to having an eating disorder, have also spawned a new, diet-related complaint: food allergies. In 1990, the model Mandy Smith's weight dropped to just five and a half stone following the collapse of her marriage to Rolling Stone Bill Wyman. The tabloid newspapers suggested she must be anorexic, and indeed she looked it. But Ms Smith claimed she was not anorexic; she had lost weight due to a yeast infection. There is no reason to doubt Ms Smith's explanation: following treatment for her problem, she regained weight fairly rapidly. But since then, many young women with anorexic-thin figures claim to have numerous food allergies and never seem to achieve a healthy weight, despite following 'special' diets.

One man I know believes his girlfriend is anorexic, despite the fact that she insists she suffers from food allergies: 'If we go out for a meal, she never eats anything, because she claims to be allergic to everything on the plate. The only things she isn't allergic to are salads, vegetables and fruit – apart from bananas, which, of course, just happen to contain more calories than any other fruit. She's allergic to salad dressing and anything which is considered to be fattening. In addition to that, she eats furtively, with her hand in front of her mouth and is obsessed with drawing attention to her figure. "My legs are so thin," she'll say, as if she really hates being underweight, but it doesn't stop her spending an hour on the exercise bike every day.'

Obviously there *are* people who have food allergies which make them physically, even seriously ill (there have been several well-publicized cases where people have died after eating peanuts), but they can also serve as an excuse for someone who is trying to hide their anorexia or bulimia. Equally, there are millions of people who turn vegetarian out of concern for the treatment of animals, but vegetarianism (and being vegan) is also a good excuse for an anorexic or bulimic to eat only vegetables for Sunday lunch. And while many Christians fast occasionally for spiritual reasons, fasting provides the anorexic or bulimic Christian with the perfect excuse for avoiding a meal or snack bar proffered by church friends.

Diet *b*reakers maintains that *only* people who are advised to follow a diet or to avoid certain foods by their GP or a hospital consultant should be dieting. There is, they say, no need for anyone else to be counting calories. (Of course, there are some professions which demand that people should be lightweight: ballerinas, for example, need to diet constantly to maintain an androgynous physique, so do women gymnasts and ice skaters, and jockeys of both sexes. And, of course, the fashion industry decrees that models should be thin. Ballerinas and gymnasts have died from following starvation diets, but they have not been big names; the same with modelling. Unfortunately, it may take the death of a very prominent ballerina, model or sports star before these worlds stop insisting that their protagonists be very thin.) People who diet for reasons of fashion – whether anorexic, bulimic, restricted eaters or compulsive eaters and failed dieters – should, according to Diet *b*reakers, work at accepting their body and getting in touch with its natural hunger signals, rather than starving it or overfeeding it. That, they say, is the way to health – both in mind and body.

Of course, this is not as easy as it sounds. It takes time – and, as Ronald Rolheiser says in *The Shattered Lantern*,[2] we live in an age where we want everything right now. The voices telling dieters to stop trying to lose weight and be happy with themselves are few – and they find it hard to make themselves heard over the thousands shouting: 'Follow my diet, lose weight, be fashionably slim and all these other things shall be added unto you – admiring glances, gorgeous partner, career success, fantastic car, a £500,000 house.' For every anti-diet book or article, there are hundreds flagging another new diet which 'worked for me – it can work for you'. As Jo Ind[3] discovered, reading Susie Orbach's *Fat Is a Feminist Issue* and agreeing with all it said, was not enough – initially – to stop her dieting. At the back of Jo's mind was the niggling thought: what if Susie Orbach is wrong and I end up fatter than ever? But when Jo realized that she had nothing to lose other than the *idea* of being slim by giving up dieting, she discovered that Orbach was not wrong – and she did not end up fatter than ever. In fact, by *not* dieting, Jo Ind lost weight.

Katie agrees: 'I read various feminist works about eating disorders when I had bulimia, and felt deep down that they were right – I was covering up many feelings by bingeing and purging. They suggested that stopping purging was the first way to break the cycle, and of course I put on heaps more weight because I was still overeating. Eventually, I stopped eating compulsively – but it took a long time, and I shed a lot of tears along the way. The feminists were right though – when I knew *why* I overate, I was able to stop. I learned to eat when I was hungry and to eat what I wanted at that moment. It was no use, for example, to eat a yoghurt if I really wanted a chocolate bar – if I tried that, I would end up eating both. When I found my natural appetite, my body found it's natural weight – and I am happier and healthier than I have ever been before.'

How *does* it work though, really? How can someone who overeats compulsively several times each day come to the point where they eat only through hunger? How can someone who maintains a strict low-calorie diet to make sure their body is always a certain shape learn to allow themselves more food and accept a higher weight? How can someone who regularly vomits up their meals stop doing so, knowing if they do they will gain weight and be a few more inches away from what society tells them is the 'ideal shape'? How can a five stone anorexic who thinks she is fat accept that she will look better and be healthier if she gains four stones? How can the ninety-eight per cent of British women who diet shut out the messages telling them that they will only be attractive and lovable if they are as thin as Kate Moss?

How *can* anyone take on board Jesus' instruction in Luke 12 – 'Do not worry about your life, what you will eat, or about your body, what you will wear. For life is more than food and the body more than clothing' – when so many people's lives revolve around their food intake, and when clothes are mass-manufactured and our bodies have to fit them, rather than the other way around?

9 Listening to Our Body Signals

So, whether you eat or drink, or whatever you do, do everything for the glory of God.

1 Corinthians 10.31

In literature prepared especially for International No Diet Day, Diet *b*reakers provides a 'list of ten good reasons to ditch that diet'. They are:

10. Diets Do Not Work. Even if you lose weight, you will probably gain it all back, and you might gain more than you lost.

9. Diets Are Expensive. If you do not buy special diet products, you could save enough to get new clothes, which would improve your appearance right now.

8. Diets Are Boring. People on diets talk and think about food and practically nothing else. There is more to life.

7. Diets Do Not Necessarily Improve Your Health. Like the weight loss, health improvement is temporary. Dieting can actually cause health problems.

6. Diets Do Not Make You Beautiful. Very few people will ever look like models or film stars. Glamour is a look, not a size. You do not have to be thin to look attractive.

5. Diets Are Not Sexy. If you want to feel and be more attractive, take care of your body and your appearance. Feeling healthy makes you look your best.

4. Diets Can Turn into Eating Disorders. The obsession to be thin can lead to anorexia, bulimia, compulsive eating and compulsive exercising.

3. Diets Can Make You Afraid of Food. Food nourishes us, and gives us pleasure. Dieting can make food seem like your enemy, and can deprive you of all the positive things about food.

2. Diets Can Rob You of Your Energy. If you want to lead a full and active life, you need good nutrition, and enough food to meet your body's needs.

And, according to Diet *b*reakers, the number one reason to give up dieting is:

1. Learning to Love and Accept Yourself just as you are will give you self-confidence, better health and a sense of well-being that will last a lifetime.

Diet *b*reakers' belief that people should learn to love and accept themselves as they are is something which the Bible advocates. But, as Emma points out, it is difficult for many people to do this when they feel fat: 'When I was eating compulsively, I loathed myself. I thought I would have to lose lots of weight before I could begin to accept myself. The more I tried and failed to diet, the worse I felt. People would say to me "God loves you even if you are fat" which I knew was true, but it didn't help. He would have loved me just the same if I were slim – and *I* would have felt better.

'But actually, when I made the decision to stop dieting and concentrate on not eating compulsively, my weight dropped – slowly, but this time I never regained it. For years I had starved myself when I was hungry and stuffed myself when I was full, but when I learned to eat when I was hungry and not eat when I was full, my problems with food – as well as my weight – ebbed away.'

Unfortunately, the majority of Western adults eat for many reasons other than the simple fact they are hungry. They eat through habit (breakfast *always* at seven thirty, lunch *always* at one, dinner *always* at six), to be sociable (I'll have dessert if you do), for comfort or to annihilate certain feelings. Similarly, the majority of Western adults who deliberately skip a meal or refuse a snack do so not because they feel comfortably full, but because they want to lose weight. None of this is healthy. Hunger and fullness are natural feelings and should be satisfied in a natural way. Eating when you are hungry and saying 'No' to food when you are full should be as natural as falling asleep when you are tired and going to the toilet when you need to.

Our culture makes it hard for people to respond naturally to the promptings of their stomach. People are expected to eat a huge Sunday lunch because, well, it is Sunday lunch. People are expected to be downright gluttonous at Christmas because 'it is Christmas, after all'. Anyone who persistently ignores the signals their body gives them by eating when they are not hungry is bound to lose touch with what their body needs. Similarly, dieters who eat crispbread and cottage cheese for lunch and spend the afternoon determinedly ignoring hunger pangs are out of touch with their bodies' needs.

It is interesting to compare an adult's relationship with food, hunger and fullness to a preschool child's. Children have a healthy eat-to-live attitude towards food, at least until their parents and other grown-ups teach them otherwise! When a child gets up each morning, their first thought – unlike an adult's – is not about whether they would like cornflakes or buttered toast for breakfast. They well may be more interested in playing with their Captain Scarlet models or Barbie doll, or their Lego. They may quickly become so absorbed in what they are doing that breakfast put in front of them by their parents – 'Eat your breakfast first, then you can play with your toys' – is an unwelcome intrusion.

Children are also attuned to how much food they need. They will eat as many cornflakes as they want, drop the spoon into the bowl and return to Captain Scarlet or whoever they are playing with. Their hunger is satisfied; now they want to do something more interesting, even if their parents are pressing them to 'Finish them all, there's a good girl/boy.' Compare this happy state of affairs with the relationship so many adults – especially women – have with food. Jodie, an anorexic, says her whole life revolves around her daily intake: 'I have half a grapefruit for breakfast, an apple for lunch and an orange for tea. I fill up with endless mugs of black coffee. I live for when it's time for me to eat.' Katie remembers being so hooked on food that nothing else interested her: 'The first thing I would think about when I woke up was *food*. Breakfast for me could be anything between a half-grapefruit and a whole loaf of bread, toasted and spread with butter. I had no hobbies, no interests. Food was everything.' Marie, a compulsive eater, says: 'I put so much energy into planning my weight-loss diets and follow them methodically for days. All I think about is my next meal, what I'm going to eat next.' Jane says: 'However much I'm enjoying a meal I have to leave something on the plate – otherwise I feel so guilty about eating it all.'

Anyone who diets – for whatever reason – can learn a lot by watching children and observing how they instinctively know when they are full and how food is not the focus of their life. Many children remain in a happy eat-when-hungry-stop-when-full state for years. Others, unfortunately, can become very young casualties of adults' foolishness. Three years ago, I shared a train carriage with a young mother and her four-year-old daughter. The child fascinated me because she was extremely fat and because she was incredibly greedy. Her mother had bought her a large Casey Jones hamburger to eat on the train and she shrieked for it until it was put into her hand. She devoured it greedily, then proceeded to eat sweets for the remainder of the journey. The mother may not have thought that she was overfeeding her, but it was clear that a playground nickname of 'Fatty' and the potential for becoming eating-disordered were already on the horizon.

Finding Your Natural Hunger

'Once I allowed myself to eat when I was hungry and stopped eating when I was full. I found my natural weight,' says Katie. 'It wasn't as low as when I wasn't eating very much, but it wasn't anywhere near as high as when I was bingeing every day. I'm happy with my weight now – I don't have to diet to maintain it, and I've stopped worrying about it. All dieting does is make you think about food all the time.'

Katie is right. Anyone who tries to lose weight always craves the food the diet sheet says they should not have. This is perhaps natural human rebellion. A friend of my mother's was put on a special diet for health reasons, and was told one of the things she must avoid was fizzy pop. My mother's friend loathed fizzy pop and never drank it – but the minute it became *verboten* she craved it. To stop craving a particular food, people must give themselves permission to eat it (unless they have been told to avoid it for medical reasons). There is nothing wrong with someone eating fish and chips or chocolate, as long as it is in moderation. It is when fish and chips are eaten every other day that they pose a health risk.

To move back towards normal eating, dieters must make the decision to stop slimming, and to learn to respond appropriately to feelings of hunger and fullness. This, like any other worthwhile achievement in life, takes time and patience. Nothing really worthwhile was ever accomplished within a short space of time, whatever the media may imply. Those sporting champions who become overnight stars at the Olympics have spent at least ten years training several hours a day six days a week for those few seconds of glory.

Dieters' main fear is that *not* dieting will make them fat or fatter. When people work with their body, not against it, by eating when they are hungry and not out of boredom, fear, unhappiness or some other reason, they will not become overweight. Those who are overweight to begin with are overweight because they are overeating. By eating normally, the pounds will slowly drop off, until natural weight is achieved. People who are underweight *will* gain some weight – but they will not become fat. They will gradually gain weight until their natural body weight is reached. Natural body weight is far healthier than an unnatural low or high one, and the person will feel more energetic, and look healthier and more attractive. Another added bonus is that when people get in touch with their body, as well as their emotions and life experiences, they come to a self-knowledge and understanding which too few folk possess. 'I really know now *how* I'm going to react to certain situations, and how best to cope with them,' says Emma.

People who are out of touch with natural feelings of hunger and fullness will find it helpful to watch how much those who *do* eat in a healthy way actually eat. Katie tried this: 'Most folk, it seemed, had a couple of slices of toast for breakfast, sandwiches for lunch, perhaps with a packet of crisps or a yoghurt or apple, and something like shepherd's pie for dinner with ice-cream or fruit afterwards, and maybe a biscuit in the evening before bedtime. I tried to keep to that kind of normal regime.' Of course, people have different metabolisms, as Katie discovered: 'I found myself getting hungry between meals – *really* hungry, my stomach rumbled! So I learnt to allow myself a snack, like a chocolate bar or a couple of biscuits. It took about a year for me to learn how much food my body needed.'

A rumbling stomach is a sure sign that a person is hungry – but it takes time to learn how intense that hunger is. Initially, some people find it helpful to eat small amounts in response to hunger – and to eat another small amount a little later if hunger pangs continue. Fullness is harder to detect, but can be helped by having a break between courses – when the main course has had a little time to digest, it is easier to judge whether a pudding is really needed.

It is important that non-dieters eat only when they are sitting at the table or in a restaurant and café. Eating on the run between work and home or in the high street confuses the body's signals. If people are tired on their way home, they do not lie down in a shop doorway and catch a few hours' sleep. If they need the toilet on the way home, they do not squat in the street (at least not in the West!) – so there is no real reason why people cannot wait until they are in the proper place before they eat. That way, the snack is likely to be much more enjoyable.

Finding Emotional Fulfilment

However much a person may try to only eat when they are hungry, they are unlikely to succeed in the long-term if they still need food as an emotional outlet. Katie says: 'When I stopped bingeing and my weight settled down after years of yo-yoing I felt great. But because I'd never confronted the *causes* of my eating disorder, just the physical side, I *still* felt inadequate at work, inadequate socially, inadequate as a person. I no longer ate to annihilate my feelings, but I started to drink increasingly heavily. In the end, I plucked up courage to go for counselling and open up about the way I felt about myself.'

The reasons *why* a person feels a need to binge on huge amounts of food or to keep their body below a certain weight need to be confronted and challenged if there is to be any real improvement. This often proves the stumbling block. 'I know I'm unhappy in my marriage, but I don't feel I can get out of it,' says Doris. 'My only comfort comes from food.' Doris's unhappiness plus the fact she feels powerless to change anything means that she is likely to continue to eat compulsively.

People have numerous reasons for feeling unhappy – perhaps they feel awkward socially, maybe they think they are ugly, maybe they are frustrated at work. Perhaps they feel their lives are not their own, because they are caring for someone who is elderly or sick. Maybe they are single and lonely. Maybe they are widowed, grieving and lonely. Maybe they are married and lonely. Maybe their marriage is unhappy, even violent, but they feel trapped in it – because they have nowhere to go, because they believe that divorce is a sin against God, because they are concerned at the effect of separation on their children. Whatever the reason, comforting oneself with food or starving oneself to flaunt a 'Please notice me' figure is not likely to change the situation. Even where there is no real prospect of a change in circumstances, unhappiness needs to be voiced. Counsellors can help people to look at the situation differently, and also to find new ways of coping with stress.

There is a saying that nobody can understand another person's problems unless they have experienced them themselves. Most Western countries have a number of organizations which help people with eating disorders (see Chapter 10 for information on UK-based ones). They usually offer support groups, where eating-disordered people can meet others who are battling with similar food problems. By talking to others with the same problem, they can help each other to find new strategies for recovery, and no longer feel they are the only person in the world who has difficulties with food. These organizations often offer opportunities for one-to-one counselling, or can refer people to a local counselling centre, where they will be able to explore and talk through the underlying reasons for their disorder in private.

Additionally, people with eating disorders often put off doing things they would like to do – because they feel fat or want to wait until they are better. It is important that people start to do these things *while* they return to normal eating. It will give them a new, creative outlet and they will have less time to spend worrying about themselves or about food.

Finding Your Natural Appetite

Hunger, of course, is different from appetite. Hunger is a growling in the stomach, appetite is salivating at the mouth. A person may not feel especially hungry, but the smell of freshly baked bread can make them long for the taste of a crusty, wholemeal loaf. People who are trying to give up feasting and fasting will find their challenge a lot easier if they eat the foods they really want when they are hungry. As Marie, who is trying to stop eating compulsively, says: 'If, when I feel hungry, I want a Mars bar, I eat a Mars bar. If I feel hungry and fancy a Chinese takeaway, I buy a Chinese takeaway. If I feel hungry and fancy lasagne, I have lasagne. And I feel satisfied on two counts – because I've eaten when I'm hungry and because I've eaten what I want.'

This strategy also worked for Jo Ind. If she felt hungry, she would ask herself, 'Is this a fish-and-chips-eaten-in-the-newspaper-made-soggy-with-vinegar kind of hungry? Is it a fresh-crispy-salad-with-soft-cottage-cheese-and-a-newly-baked-granary-roll kind of want?' Before eating, Jo carefully considered what she wanted to taste, the texture she wanted to feel.

Of course, both Marie and Jo Ind are single women, with only themselves to please, foodwise. People who are married and perhaps have children to feed may argue that satisfying their own appetite is not so easy. However, the majority of people who diet prepare a separate, low-calorie meal for themselves anyway. What's the difference in making a separate bacon sandwich from preparing a special recipe-for-one from the *F-Plan Diet*? And it is likely that when an ex-dieter prepares herself or himself a tasty meal for a change, instead of a fat-free, calorie-free, taste-free one, maybe their children would not mind having a portion of it too!

People who are out of touch with their hunger and appetite may initially have trouble recognizing the food they really want – and may also struggle to allow themselves to have it. 'Tonight, for tea, I wanted pizza and chips, but I made myself have a yoghurt instead,' says Tania, a 20-year-old recovering anorexic. Again, patience is needed – it takes a long time for an eating disorder to develop, and getting back in touch with your natural appetite will not happen overnight.

Accepting Your Natural Shape

Everybody is different. People have different skin colour, different hair colour, different shoe sizes. People are different heights. Some people have blue eyes, others brown, others grey, others green. Some people freckle, some people get a suntan, some people have moles. Some people are more intelligent than others, some people have more common sense than others, some people have better-paid jobs than others. Some people come close to God by reading books on theology, others come close to God in a charismatic-style church. Some people are good at sport, others are so uncoordinated that they can never catch a ball. Some people are funny, other people are always serious. Everyone is different and it would be boring if we were all the same.

Similarly, everyone's body shape is different, and no matter how much we may diet, how much we overeat, we cannot alter our natural, God-given body shape. I have a friend who is the same height as I am and weighs the same as I do. But nobody would think so, because our bodies are so different. She is straight-up-and-down, not a hip or bust in sight; I am curvy, with a small waist and a D-cup bra. If we both gained a stone or lost a stone, we would still retain our own, individual body shape. There is nothing either of us can do to change it.

The singer Karen Carpenter starved herself to death trying to change her body shape. She went down to five and a half stone, but still believed her hips were too big.

She yearned for the straight-up-and-down figure beloved by the media. Karen Carpenter loved music and had eclectic tastes: she liked the Beatles, the Rolling Stones, country music and classical music. She appreciated good music, regardless of its genre, and would not have said one style was better than another. But she could not accept that one body shape was not better than another.

Most people feel like that – perhaps not as deeply as she did, but they feel it all the same. And it is important that, collectively, individuals learn to accept their own, unique body shape rather than make repeated, futile attempts to transform their body into something regarded as 'fashionable'.

Take Some Exercise

Several years ago, I got chatting to a man at a sports event. He looked very fit and healthy, and told me he swam every morning and played golf or tennis every other day. He looked about fifty and I assumed he had taken early retirement. Incredibly, he turned out to be over seventy.

Most people today lead sedentary lives – working all day in an office, driving to and from work and to the shops. The UK Sports Council claims that lack of exercise is the reason so many Britons have become overweight. They advocate taking regular exercise in addition to eating a healthy, balanced diet.

Exercise does not have to be playing football or pounding the pavements. The Sports Council states that the best form of exercise is walking – walking briskly to and from work on a regular basis will make a difference to your muscle tone and energy levels. A walk can be taken at your own pace, it can be solitary or with family and friends. A long country walk on a Saturday or Sunday afternoon will blow the cobwebs away and is terrific exercise.

There are lots of exercise classes to choose from and gyms to work-out in, as well as plenty of competitive sports to try. It is important not to become obsessive about exercise or to feel you *have* to work out at the same time every day. A few hours spent exercising every week will make all the difference to your levels of fitness and to your sense of well-being.

Find Spiritual Fulfilment

Ronald Rolheiser states, in his book, *The Shattered Lantern*,[1] that people are so pressurized today that they have become unaware of God's presence in everyday life. And while that is something which one imagines applies only to non-Christians, the fact is that many Christians too have become unaware of God's presence. This can happen when the I'm-busy-I-want-action-now philosophy spills over into the Christian life. Working at prayer, spending lengthy periods in prayer or reading the Bible are all time-consuming and in the almost-twenty-first century Western world many people have lost that kind of patience. Rolheiser also argues that some sections of the church have taken away God's mystery and holiness and have made him so familiar that that familiarity can lead to contempt. This can cause people to lose their faith.

Too often in the church, people are discouraged from voicing what they believe by others who want them to toe a particular denominational 'party line'. While some people will fit very happily into one particular worshipping tradition, others may find it stultifyingly narrow. Frustrations and doubts about particular doctrine can all too easily lead to frustrations and doubts about God. Some people turn from God completely when all they probably needed was to find a different place of worship, where they felt comfortable, and free to state where they disagreed on doctrine. God is much bigger than all the Christian traditions put together. No one of them is absolutely right, but each of them has something valid to say.

Looking into what causes an eating disorder – or any

other emotional problem – can often lead a person to question some of their preconceptions about themselves, their lifestyle, society, the world and about God. Such questioning often leads an atheist or agnostic to discover God's existence and to commit themselves to him. But it can also lead previously committed Christians to question church dogma and even the existence of God. It is at this point when those questioning their former firm beliefs need the love and support, not the condemnation or even advice, of their fellow churchgoers. Emma questioned her faith throughout her recovery from compulsive eating, and says: 'In retrospect, it was narrow expressions of Christianity which frustrated me – I still believed in and worshipped God. My faith, as a result of that "spiritual crisis" is broader now, and I feel I have greater sympathy towards others who struggle, both with faith and with addictions like an eating disorder.'

Helpful Hints

1. For Anorexics

- Anorexia is more than a physical problem; it is a sign that something is very wrong. If you are serious about recovery, then it is important to ask yourself why you want to lose weight and why being very thin means so much to you.
- *Talk to your GP about your eating disorder. They may be able to refer you to an eating disorders unit or hospital. If, for some reason, you do not want to talk to a doctor, contact a local therapy or counselling centre, or find out about local support groups for anorexia (national organizations which can help are discussed in Chapter 10).*
- Try to eat meals with other people – even if, at first, you only want to pick at half a grapefruit. Watch how

much they eat. Note that the food is not the main focus of the meal: the conversation is (or should be). Try to join in conversations and to enjoy what you are eating.

• *Recovery does not mean instantly going from eating virtually nothing to tucking into a hearty breakfast, lunch and dinner! Build up your food intake slowly – with an extra piece of fruit, some milk in your coffee, or butter on your bread. Eating too much after a period of restricted eating can be dangerous because of the sudden swelling of the stomach lining.*

• Work at changing your beliefs about body shape. In your experience, has losing weight improved your lifestyle? Has it made you happier, popular, more successful like it was supposed to in the glossy ads? Work at being you – at accepting *your* unique body shape, *your* unique way of perceiving things, *your* unique personality.

2. For Bulimics

• Nobody becomes bulimic if they are happy with their lives. What is bothering you? Are your emotional needs being met? Do you feel fulfilled by your role in life? Are you fulfilled spiritually – even apparently mature, committed Christians can feel unfulfilled deep down.

• *Resolve to stop purging, even if initially you will put on some weight. Purging is extremely harmful, and by deciding not to do it, the first link in the binge-purge-starve-binge chain will be broken. It is not easy, but after a while the binges will become smaller and less frequent, and you will gradually return to a healthy, natural weight.*

• Decide to stop dieting. Instead, eat three healthy meals each day. Listen to your body – it will tell you when it is hungry. Try to work out which food you really want to eat.

• *Identify foods which lead you to binge – many*

bulimics claim that if they eat cereal, bread or dried fruit they are likely to overeat. Avoid those foods for a while and see if the binges stop. You may be able to return to them once you are free of the compulsion to binge.

• Identify situations which cause you to binge. Stress, tiredness, frustration, loneliness, boredom, unhappiness, failure, even success, can lead a person to fly to the fridge. Try to think of ways of handling these emotions rather than by bingeing.

3. For Compulsive Eaters

• Compulsive eating is very similar to bulimia – the only real difference is that compulsive eaters do not purge. Therefore, the hints for bulimics wishing to stop dieting and learn to accept their body, are worth reading and acting upon.

• *Whenever you find yourself craving food, ask yourself what you really need. Are you really, physically hungry? Or do you need something else – reassurance, a hug, help with a problem, an excuse to put off something you do not want to do? Try to resolve that need without turning to food.*

• Always put your food on a plate and eat it slowly, making yourself aware of its texture and taste. Never eat directly from the packet or wrapper or while you are standing up.

• *Accept that your problem is to do with eating not with weight. Eating compulsively when you are not hungry is harmful to your body and this situation will be exacerbated, not altered, by trying to follow the latest fad diet.*

4. For Restricted Eaters

• Although you may not be as thin as an anorexic, your problem is similar in that, by maintaining a rigid diet, you are keeping your body at a weight which is unrealistic and unnatural for you. Ask yourself what would happen if you were half a stone heavier – would you lose your job? Would your partner stop loving you? Would you really get called 'Fatty' if you were a natural, healthy weight? (Giving up rigid control over your food intake does not mean you will blow up like a balloon.)

- *Ask yourself which is more important – your health or being fashionably slim? If it's the latter, then you need to change your outlook on life. And remember that very slim people often look increasingly haggard the older they get, and that a thin, pinched face is far from attractive.*
- Think about the effects your constant dieting and figure-consciousness may be having on your children or grandchildren. Do you really want the next generation putting themselves through agonies in the name of fashion?

Because all eating disorders are interrelated, a compulsive eater or bulimic will find advice for anorexics or restricted eaters helpful and vice versa. The overweight compulsive eater may seem light years away from a starving, emaciated anorexic, but this is not the case. Both are using food to express unresolved emotional conflict.

10 Finding Help and Support

No testing has overtaken you that is not common to everyone. God is faithful, and he will not let you be tested beyond your strength, but with your testing he will also provide the way out so that you may be able to endure it.

1 Corinthians 10.13

Support Groups

It *is* possible to overcome an eating problem alone. But it is easier to do it with the help of other people, particularly those who have been through or are going through similar difficulties themselves. This is why many dieters have benefited from attending a local support group.

In the United Kingdom, local and regional support groups have been set up by the four main national eating disorders organisations (the Eating Disorders Association, Anorexia and Bulimia Care, Diet *b*reakers and Overeaters Anonymous) and several more have been established by bodies like the Women's Therapy Centre in London. Such groups are usually small (up to 20 people) and members are encouraged to contribute to the subjects discussed at each meeting.

Interestingly, those topics are not always connected with food – at least not directly. I sat in on one local support group which was discussing possible subjects for its fortnightly meetings over the following three months. The topics suggested by the (mainly anorexic or bulimic) members included overcoming fears, being assertive, how to communicate with other people and how to communicate with God. Food as a discussion point was not mentioned; though, of course, all the things the members wanted to discuss had – for them – somehow become tied up with food. Members are encouraged to go along to meetings until – and after – they are better.

The group leader who ran the meeting I sat in on told me: 'It is good to have people at different stages of their eating disorder meeting on a regular basis, because they not only encourage each other to get better, but they also – involuntarily – *discourage* each other from getting worse. For example, we have one bulimic group member who is in her forties and has been either anorexic or bulimic since she was eighteen. There are a couple of 18-year-olds in the group – one anorexic, one bulimic – who look at her and say to themselves: "I don't still want to be feeling and thinking like that when *I'm* forty." And, of course, the sufferer who is forty is really putting a lot of effort into trying to recover, because she doesn't want to see anorexics and bulimics young enough to be her children come along and end up recovered and healthy while she's still there struggling.'

Obviously, many people find it difficult to pluck up courage to attend an eating disorders group – for a variety of reasons. 'I didn't want to go, because I thought everybody in it would be thinner than me and would look at me and think: "*She* doesn't have an eating disorder",' says Emma, a compulsive eater. 'But actually, when I did attend one, I found the members were at all different weights and stages of their varying disorders.' John, a teacher who suffers from bulimia, explains: 'I was reluctant to go because I thought I'd be the only bloke! Actually, I wasn't – there was another one, a compulsive eater. But actually, it was just as easy to relate to women who shared my problems with food.'

Doris, who has attended several slimming clubs down the years, says: 'I wouldn't go, because I don't like sharing my problems with other people. After all, they get you to come straight out with it, "My name's Doris and I can't stop eating", and talk about why you have a problem. I think your private life should be private.' And yet those people who have decided to open up about their secret feelings, fears and emotions rather than annihilating them by eating or starving, have discovered – unlike Doris – that their problems with food have gradually gone away.

They have also discovered that, by attending support groups, they have made new friends. 'I made several friends through the group meetings I attended, some of them anorexic, some bulimic, some compulsive eaters, and some who were not anorexic but had anorexic attitudes,' says Heidi. 'We all had two things in common: we loved and feared food and we wanted to be super-thin. But we discovered we had more common interests than that – we shared views about politics and Christianity, and had experienced problems with members of the opposite sex. Somehow, if you can open up about the horrible aspects of your eating disorder – such as how much you eat and being sick – then you can talk intimately about *anything*. I am closer to my friends who have had eating disorders than I am to any group of people, including those from church – because, with eating disordered people, you can open up about *anything*, and there's no condemnation, nobody is shocked. They've usually done just the same things themselves – and feel just the same way about them as you do.'

Counselling

Everyone, at some point in their life, needs somebody to talk to, somebody who is outside the situation, somebody who is prepared to listen, rather than interrupt with: 'Well, if *I* were you, *I* would . . .'

People who struggle with food and weight problems usually do need to offload – not only about the physical aspect of their disorder, but about what is really bugging them deep down. Those who have become badly anorexic and bulimic are often referred by their GP to a psychiatrist or psychologist. The majority of people with eating problems do not need that – but talking to a counsellor on a one-to-one, regular basis has often proved extremely helpful.

Details of local counselling centres can be found in libraries, telephone directories, at Citizens Advice Bureaux, from the Eating Disorders Association and Anorexia and Bulimia Care or from GPs. Counselling sessions are generally weekly and last for one hour. Fees are usually on a sliding scale, according to income. Before signing up for counselling sessions, people should ensure that the counsellor they will be seeing is properly qualified.

Most present-day counselling is based on the teaching of psychologist Carl Rogers, and is known as 'Rogerian' or 'non-directive' counselling. The emphasis is on self-acceptance: people with a low sense of self-worth or who feel they are unattractive are encouraged to accept themselves for who they are – physically, intellectually and emotionally. The counsellor's role is not to advise: it is to listen to what the counsellee is saying, and allow them to draw their own conclusions about why their life is in a mess and what they can do to improve it. Rachel, who is seeing a counsellor about her compulsive eating, says: 'The thing that struck me, in the first session, was that my counsellor didn't speak. I had an hour in which to talk. Every time I stopped talking, she would say "Go on" or "Can you expand on that?" I realized I felt uncomfortable about talking for so long. Usually, at home, people always cut right across what I was saying, and suddenly I thought: "What *right* do they have to do that?"'

Some Christian organizations and churches offer counselling, and Christians with eating problems may prefer a God-centred approach. Christian counsellors stress that God accepts people as they are, regardless of whether they are conventionally attractive. They encourage counsellees to live their lives according to Christ's values rather than the world's. As with secular counselling, it is important to check that the counsellor is qualified. There have been too many incidents of enthusiastic Christians offering so-called counselling based on 'words of knowledge' on medical problems they know nothing about. Often, unwittingly, they have actually exacerbated their 'counsellee's' problems. A list of accredited Christian counsellors can be obtained from the Association of Christian Counsellors, Kings House, 175 Wokingham Road, Reading, RG6 1LT.

Many people are reluctant to seek counselling, sometimes because they do not wish to be categorized as a 'person with problems' and sometimes because they feel that they will be wasting the counsellor's time. Christian psychologist Ray White, who runs counselling courses in the south of England, insists that anyone who believes they might benefit from counselling should not be afraid to ask for it: 'It is far better to think you have a need and then be told you're OK and perfectly normal than the other way round,' he says. He stresses that anyone with a problem which impinges on their lives should seek counselling: 'People who are afraid of everyday things, such as eating in public, should do something about it. Being fearful is not what the Lord wants.'

Helpful Organizations

Most Western countries now have organizations which offer help, understanding and hope to people with eating disorders. Almost all of them run a network of self-help groups and offer one-to-one counselling. I would encourage anyone who recognizes that they have a problem with their approach to food and weight to contact an organization which can help them. People resident in Britain can seek help and support from the organizations listed in this chapter. Eating-disordered people living in other Western countries will find information about similar organizations in their local library or telephone directory.

The Eating Disorders Association (EDA)

Established in 1989, following a merger between Anorexic Aid and Anorexic Family Aid, EDA hit the headlines in 1992, when Princess Diana addressed its annual conference. EDA offers support to anorexics and bulimics in the form of literature (including a newsletter, which looks at eating disorders from various angles, including media pressures, elderly sufferers and male sufferers); a telephone helpline; regional support groups (run by former anorexics and bulimics); and a list of local eating disorders units and counsellors.

EDA also provides information for families and friends of eating disordered people, indicating ways in which they can help the sufferer return to a healthy relationship with food.

Address: Eating Disorders Association, Sackville Place, 44 Magdalen Street, Norwich, Norfolk NR3 1JU.

Anorexia and Bulimia Care (ABC)

ABC is a Christian organization, which began in 1983 as a support group for anorexics and bulimics in the Ormskirk area of England. In 1989, it amalgamated with a small organization based in the south of England and is now a national charity, with hundreds of sufferers on its list.

ABC provides help to sufferers (including compulsive eaters) by pairing them with a committed Christian 'carer' (often an ex-sufferer) and sending them an information pack about eating disorders. Information packs are also available for relatives and friends, and churches. There are some regional support groups. All ABC members (whether sufferers, carers or other interested parties) receive a national newsletter.

Address: Anorexia and Bulimia Care (Northern office), 15 Fernhurst Gate, Aughton, Lancs L39 5ED; (Southern office), Arisaig, Back Lane, Monks Eleigh, Suffolk IP7 7BA.

Diet breakers

Diet *b*reakers was set up in 1991, by a woman called Mary Evans Young, who had spent twenty-three years dieting and worrying about her weight until attending a series of self-development classes. Now, Diet *b*reakers organizes International No Diet Day (each May) as well as running special ten-week programmes for women called, 'You count, calories don't'.

The programme encourages women to listen to their natural hunger signals and to find emotional satisfaction from other areas of their lives. Diet *b*reakers also acts as a pressure group by challenging the diet industry, raising public awareness of what it calls 'the tyranny of thinness' and giving talks and workshops on the health and social risks of dieting.

Address: Diet *b*reakers, Barford St Michael, Banbury, Oxon OX15 0UA.

Overeaters Anonymous

A foodie version of Alcoholics Anonymous, based on the twelve-step programme. Bulimics and compulsive eaters attend regional group meetings, and are usually paired with another overeater, whom they can phone at times when they are tempted to binge. Following the twelve-step plan, overeaters admit they are powerless over food and that their life has become unmanageable. They recognize that only a Power which is higher than themselves can restore them to sanity around food. They turn their lives over to that Power, ask it to remove defects of character, and state their willingness to make amends to people they have harmed in the past. They also promise to improve conscious contact with that Power by prayer and meditation.

The approach can be off-putting to some Christian overeaters, because they are unsure who the other group members are praying to. However, many Christians have stated that following the twelve steps has not only helped them to overcome overeating, but has also strengthened their relationship with Jesus Christ.

Address: Overeaters Anonymous, PO Box 19, Stretford, Manchester M32 9EB.

All four of the above organizations have achieved much success in helping people with eating problems to develop a healthy approach to food and weight. Generally, the help and support offered by the Eating Disorders Association and Anorexia and Bulimia Care (particularly the latter) is more likely to appeal to younger people – for example, teenage girls and eating-disordered people in their early to mid-twenties. Equally generally, the approach of Diet *b*reakers and Overeaters Anonymous is more likely to appeal to older eating-disordered people, from the late twenties upwards, and particularly the thirty- and forty-somethings. Details of other organizations and support groups can be found in local libraries.

11 How the Church Can Help

But when you thus sin against members of your family, and wound their conscience when it is weak, you sin against Christ. Therefore, if food is a cause of their failing, I will never eat meat, so that I may not cause one of them to fall.

1 Corinthians 8.12–13

How many churches do you know where the leaders invite alcoholic members of their congregation out for a few beers? How many churches make drugs available to addicts within the community? Such things, we know, simply would not happen; Christians *help* addicts, not encourage them. And yet, after Sunday services, at special church events and anniversaries, and during home group meetings, Christians persistently lay out tables of tempting goodies before other Christians – and non-Christians – who may be struggling with an eating disorder.

It could be argued that not everybody has an eating problem, so why should the majority of people miss out on refreshments simply because two or three people in the congregation have a problem with food? Rachel, who finds all food-centred occasions difficult, states: 'I appreciate that not everybody feels the urge to binge when there is food around. But not everybody feels the urge to get drunk when there is alcohol around. So why don't church garden parties offer beer and wine? I know that too much alcohol can make a person a danger to other people as well as themselves – but those who cannot control themselves around food are harming themselves too, physically and psychologically.'

Anthony Campolo,[1] in his highly sensitive chapter on 'Gluttony' in *Seven Deadly Sins* recalls how a thirty-something, 300-pound man came face to face with his reflection in a mirror at a New Year's Eve party:

> As midnight approached, he thought of the jokes people had made all evening at his expense. He thought of how he had pretended to play along with the painful cheap shots he had endured. None of the women at the party had sought his companionship, even though he was alone. Everybody, he thought, regarded him as a merry buffoon, and as he saw his image in the mirror, the attitudes of the others seemed justified. This sad fat man who covered up his hurt with jolly laughter told me that the only thing that kept him from killing himself that night was his fear of death and judgement.

According to figures supplied by the Eating Disorders Association, anorexia and bulimia have one of the highest mortality rates of all psychiatric illnesses; over ten per cent of registered sufferers die, either from the effects of starvation or by committing suicide. Additionally, the millions of people in the Western world who are clinically obese are shortening their lives through vulnerability to heart disease, diabetes, stroke and certain cancers. People who yo-yo diet and are constantly losing and regaining weight also put their long-term health at risk, as do those who keep their weight deliberately low by persistent slimming.

As Anthony Campolo's story shows, eating and weight problems often cause extreme psychological trauma, but non-eating disordered people – including those in the church – seem blissfully unaware of it. Anyone who is larger or smaller than average always seems to be fair game for so-called funny or sarcastic remarks. Christians who would never dream of saying 'Go on, have a beer pal, it won't hurt you' to an alcoholic struggling to stay on the wagon, will not balk at quipping a so-called joke to someone struggling with their attitude to food.

Many years ago, I went on a trip to the north of England with some members of a church I attended. On the way, we stopped for coffee at a motorway service station. A plump young woman of about twenty, who had been on and off diets for about two years, chose a chocolate éclair to eat with her coffee. One of the church leaders – a man in his early fifties – sat next to her and, without saying anything, cut her éclair in half and transferred one piece to his own plate. When the rest of us – including the one who had bought the éclair – stared in disbelief, he shrugged his shoulders and said: 'Just trying to help a sister with a weight problem!' It may have been a coincidence, but it was not too long before the 'sister with a weight problem' stopped attending church.

The church needs to be more sensitive towards people who may have food-related problems. Christians are supposed to be 'in the world, but not of it', but too often they restrict that command to just a handful of things – such as not sleeping with one's prospective partner before marriage, not having a flutter on the National Lottery or the Cheltenham Gold Cup, and not taking part in Sunday sport. But those who point the finger at the peccadilloes of others may well be flouting Christ's command themselves – by colluding with society's view that only slimness is *really* attractive; by teasing someone mercilessly about their weight; by publicly stating that confessed-bulimic Princess Diana has a much more attractive figure than the Duchess of York, by crash-dieting in the spring to wear a smaller-size bikini in the summer, or by overfeeding or underfeeding their body for emotional reasons. Some of these points may *appear* trivial, but what do children and impressionable adults discern from them?

It is interesting that the Bible does not often refer to people's appearance. The Gospels do not tell us whether Jesus was tall, hefty or thin. The New Testament does not tell us Lydia's dress size or how much Mary Magdalene weighed. All we know is that Jesus told his followers not to worry about what they ate, or about what they should wear. If he were speaking directly to contemporary society on this subject, he could well be saying: 'Don't worry if you have eaten 300 calories more than the latest best-selling diet manual says you should. Don't worry if you are not going to fit in a size-eight bikini by summer. There are more important things than that.'

Of course, that does not mean Christians should not care about their appearance or their health. There is no reason why they should not wear flattering clothes or try to eat sensibly and healthily. What Jesus is surely saying is that eating and apparel should not be all-important. If your weight is endangering your health, lose (or gain) a few pounds by all means, but do it by working with your body and *do not be obsessive*. Wear nice clothes by all means, but do not think you have to fit into a certain size just to be fashionable and acceptable, and *do not let appearance rule your life*.

The church can help to shift society's emphasis on slimness by taking a lead in affirming people for who they are and not what they look like. There is obviously nothing wrong with being beautiful and nothing wrong with having a fashionably slim figure (as long as it is natural, and not attained by rigid dieting or purging after meals). What is wrong is when people who are not at all beautiful and far from naturally slim are made to feel like inadequate failures by comparison. Many people have to cope with this in most areas of life – in the school playground, at parties and on holiday when no one from the opposite sex pays attention to them, even in their own family ('You're not as pretty as your sister, are you?') and it is sad that they should also have to cope with it in the church.

One Christian woman, Lucy, recalls a day's outing to the beach with some members of another church: 'A group of friends from John's old church invited him to join them on a day out at Rye. He asked three of us along – me, his friend Mike and my flatmate Helen. When we arrived at Rye, Helen disappeared off to the loo and John's friends were introduced to Mike and me first. When Helen reappeared, having just applied extra make-up and brushed her long blonde hair, the men were riveted. They didn't acknowledge me but they all wanted to talk to her. I was *so* angry – how *dared* they ignore me just because I wasn't stunning like Helen? It ruined the day for me.' It also spoilt relations between Lucy and the men from John's former church, because when, later on, they tried to chat to her – Helen having paired off with one of them – Lucy ignored them.

It may be a generalization, but men do seem to be much more interested in the beautiful, blonde, slim woman than they are in any other variety – God may be looking at a person's heart, but men are ogling her legs. There are some women who are only interested in very good-looking men, but generally women tend to be more attracted to the whole person – sense of humour, sensitivity to others, political persuasion and religious beliefs are much more important than looks. All this applies equally to men and women in the church. If a very attractive female newcomer appears in the congregation, the men swarm. If a not-so-attractive female newcomer appears in the congregation, the men ignore her. Women – again generally – tend to talk to all male newcomers, regardless of looks. (Maybe the fact that women outnumber men in the church by so wide a margin means they cannot be so choosy!)

The sad thing is that someone who is ignored because they are not attractive will subsequently feel even less attractive than they did before. Oversights undermine their confidence and make a person feel even less likely to want to meet new people because of possible further rejection. This should not happen in society, but it does. It certainly should not happen in the church, but it does. And concerned Christians can do something about it.

They can intervene when they notice a child being bullied or ostracized because of their appearance in the Sunday school or youth group (or anywhere else for that matter). They can make sure that every newcomer to the church is greeted properly, and made to feel included, by members of both sexes. They can try to affirm something about every person in the church. OK, one person may not be terribly good-looking, but they may be the only person who can fix a car properly, or arrange the flowers beautifully. Christians who preach in church can try to avoid making comments to do with appearance: 'Unlike me, my daughter's grown up to be very good-looking – slim, with long legs.' And to help those struggling with an eating disorder, leaders can organize regular activities which are not food-centred (see panel at the end of this chapter) and perhaps allow an eating disorders support group to meet on church premises. Churches which have regular days or half-days of prayer and fasting might consider stopping them for a while to consider whether folk are fasting only for spiritual reasons. After all, churches throughout the country are busy turning 'family worship' into 'all-age worship' to make singles and older people feel included, so why not make the effort to combat 'sizeism' and 'looksism' too?

Leaders might also consider preaching the occasional – or even frequent – sermon on the body. After all, we hear plenty of sermons on how God feels about the environment, money, politics, animals, singleness, the family and the Third World. But when did anyone ever go into church and hear the minister preaching a sermon about the way God feels about the human body? David may have praised God because he [David] was 'wonderfully and fearfully made', but the opinion of the majority of contemporary Christians goes something like this: 'I'm glad our bodies don't go to heaven with us when we die. I don't want this one!' And the majority of people who make statements like this are those who have a perfectly healthy body – it is just not fashionably slim or as straight-up-and-down as they would like it to be.

But people are brought up to be embarrassed by their bodies for reasons other than fashion. Totally natural bodily functions – like going to the toilet, or having a period, feminine itch, vaginal discharge or an erection – are embarrassing to many people and are totally unmentionable in polite Western society. Problems like incontinence are seen as embarrassing not only by the sufferer but by those around them. Bodily functions are perhaps even less mentionable within church circles than in the rest of Western society. Within some Christian circles, the sight of too much flesh is often frowned upon – low-cut dresses, mini-skirts and bikinis will be tutted at, let alone topless or nude sunbathing! In the church, the spirit is of primary importance: Christians should strive to be like Jesus, by reading the Bible and praying to him every day. The mind is of secondary importance: it is good to do well in 'A' levels and to stretch oneself intellectually (though there are some churches which frown upon this). But the body comes a poor third – it is weak and, unless controlled, can lead to sin against God.

Jo Ind's[2] book points out something which few people fully appreciate: Jesus had a body. When the Word became flesh, Jesus' body was no different to any other man's. We are told that he became tired as we do, that he needed to eat and to quench his thirst as we do. Walking for miles in scorching sunshine, he would have become hot and sweaty. We are not told that he needed to relieve himself as he journeyed, but there is no doubt that he did – however blasphemous it may seem to our minds. Additionally, Jesus was not disgusted by other people's bodies: he touched those with leprosy, and he did not balk when a woman who had been bleeding for twelve years (in a hot Middle Eastern country, well before the days of sanitary pads, toiletries and hygienic washing facilities) reached out and touched him.

Somehow the church has rejected the idea of Jesus as a real-life flesh-and-blood person – but he was. So too were all the other Bible characters, Abraham, Moses, David, Elijah, the Virgin Mary, Paul – all of them. But today's church, instead of helping people to integrate the physical, mental and spiritual, encourages Christians to believe that only one, the spiritual, is of real importance. Yet God used the body – the Word become flesh – to reveal himself to humankind.

Maybe it is time for home groups to start discussing the human body at Wednesday-night meetings: to express awe at the way the human body works on the inside; to be amazed by the complex workings of the digestive system; to marvel at the way a new human being is conceived and grows in the womb; to be really mind-blown by how the baby gets out of the womb. Christians rightly wonder at God's creative powers in forming the galaxies, the earth, mountains, lakes, rivers, trees . . . But are not our own bodies just as incredible, just as beautiful, just as intricately designed?

The Bible says that, for Christians, the body is the 'temple' of the Holy Spirit. Surely this is a very good reason for Christians to accept their own body and to look after it properly – by giving it adequate nutrition and caring for all aspects of it? As Selwyn Hughes puts it, in his book, *God Wants You Whole*,[3]

> if every Christian was to give the body its rightful care and consideration then, instead of going to heaven before our time, we would be able to share God's love with our friends and families, and the community in which we live, and thus fulfil our mission on this earth.

Churches, then, should lead the way in encouraging people to accept their body, regardless of what it looks like – and to care for it by giving it adequate nutrition. Christians should not view their body as an embarrassment, but as a gift from God. And stewardship of the God-given body is as important as stewardship of money, talents or time.

Ten Church Activities Which Do Not Involve Food

1. Rambling/walking (*during the morning or afternoon – no need to take a picnic).*

2. Sightseeing (*visit a cathedral, an old church, a National Trust house or gardens, or something of interest in your area – minus the stop at the coffee shop*).

3. Visit the theatre, cinema or a sports event (*going to watch something as a church can be fun – and there is no need to have ice-creams in the interval or munch popcorn all the way through).*

4. Go ten-pin bowling or skating.

5. Organize a treasure hunt in your region – with clues along the way and a non-food prize at the end.

6. Have tea and coffee, but not biscuits or cake, available after church services or housegroup meetings.

7. Run evening classes in crafts like cross-stitch, art, calligraphy and flower-arranging, with just coffee or tea available.

8. Take an evening boat trip along the river or canal (*again with tea or coffee only as refreshments*).

9. Have a video evening.

10. Have a brainstorming session for ideas for other non-food based activities.

12 How You Can Make a Difference

Do not, for the sake of food, destroy the work of God.

Romans 14.20

To help to change society's emphasis on slimness and prevent the next generation of eating disordered people, individuals can:

• *Stop allowing food and diet to dominate their own lives, by eating in response to natural hunger, accepting their own, unique body shape, and finding other ways of expressing emotion other than through food.*

• Write to their local MPs asking them to support any further parliamentary proposals to regulate the diet industry. MPs can be contacted at the House of Commons, Westminster, London SW1A 0AA, or at their constituency offices (local libraries and telephone directories have details).

• *Encourage everyone who has been on a diet which has failed to work to write a letter of complaint to the manufacturer or publisher. Generally people who fail to lose weight blame themselves, and their silence leads others to try a diet which does not work.*

• Write a letter of complaint to the editor of any newspaper or magazine which uses pictures of thin models to illustrate their articles, praises the trim figure of anyone who is believed to be anorexic or bulimic, carries 'miracle diet' features, or runs advertisements for weight-loss centres, pills or other slimming products which are likely to be harmful.

• *Write letters of complaint to the producer of any television programme which might encourage unhealthy attitudes towards food, diet and body image. These can include soap operas and children's programmes as well as documentaries. Programmes like BBC1's* Points of View *and Channel 4's* Right to Reply *welcome the public's opinions on programme content.*

• Write to television station managers complaining about any advertisements which indicate that only slim people are successful, or which encourage people to feel guilty about eating food.

• *Join a politically active anti-diet organization like* Diet breakers *to find out about national and local activities aimed at drawing attention to the tyranny of thinness.*

• Teach their children to accept and care for their body. Explain that starving or overfeeding the body can be harmful, just as nicotine, alcohol and drugs are harmful. Teach them to express their emotions and fears openly, rather than by using food. Remember that children learn from example, so it is no use a parent telling their children that comfort-eating is harmful if they reach for the biscuit barrel every time they are upset or bored.

• *Throw the weighing scales, diet sheets and calorie counters out of the house, and avoid family conversations centred around dieting.*

• Encourage their church to be more aware of the dangers of dieting and of the needs of eating-disordered people within the church and community. Send for Anorexia and Bulimia Care's church pack to help the minister and leaders understand what the problems are and how they can help.

• *Discourage diet-based conversations, whether at work, at church or with friends. There are surely more important things to discuss.*

• Ask friends or relatives who are dieting why they want to lose weight. Ask what difference they believe weight loss will make to their lives. Encourage them to concentrate on re-finding their natural hunger and appetite rather than trying to keep to a diet which, ultimately, is highly likely to fail.

- *Always affirm other people for what they are or the skills they have rather than what they look like.*
- Remember that *collectively* individuals can achieve a great deal. If only one person writes to a diet manufacturer, newspaper editor or television producer, nothing is likely to change. But if *everybody* who is concerned about the increase in eating disorders in society writes, then a great deal will change. Encourage any friends and relatives who share your concerns to write as well.
- *Press for better health care. Despite the fact that there are some 200,000 registered anorexics and bulimics in the UK, specialist treatment centres throughout the country can only treat about 1,500 patients each year. Write to the Health Secretary voicing your concern — the address is Department of Health, Richmond House, 79 Whitehall, London SW1A 2NS.*
- Contact Diet *b*reakers for information about the next International No Diet Day, and encourage friends, relatives and concerned Christians to take part.
- *Pray for anyone who struggles with food and weight difficulties, and for society's emphasis on thinness to come to an end.*

How to Help Someone with an Eating Disorder

Eating disorders are rife – even in the churches. If you know someone who is struggling with anorexia, bulimia, compulsive eating or who eats in a restricted way, and want to help them, remember the following tips:

- *If the eating disordered person is a Christian, do not tell them that if they were a 'real Christian' they would accept themselves as God accepts them, and the problem would not be there.*
- Do not think that only very thin people have 'real'

eating problems. Those with eating disorders come in all shapes and sizes, depending on how much they binge and purge. It is their *attitude* to food and weight which is central to the problem.

• *If you pray with an eating-disordered person, make sure you know what the problem really is. Many bulimics complain about other Christians praying for them to overcome anorexia.*

• If you live with someone with an eating problem, do not leave food around the house, hoping they will eat it. Would you leave alcohol in the house if the person was alcoholic?

• *Do not make comments about the person's appearance. 'You look well/pretty' might be construed as 'You look fat/ you've put on weight'. 'You look too thin' will suggest that the person's diet is succeeding and if they eat a little less, it will work even better!*

• Encourage the eating-disordered person to mix with other people and to pursue interests unconnected with food.

• *Praise and encourage any qualities the person has, as long as they are unconnected with food. (I once heard of a bulimic who was a talented violinist, but was banned by her church leadership from playing in the church music group until her bulimia was better, thereby proving that her relationship with God was good. She felt so humiliated by this public 'punishment' that she stopped attending church, and eventually drew away from God. She also found herself with even more time in which to binge!)*

• Do not make careless, hurtful comments like 'You needed to lose weight anyway' or 'If you're really worried about your weight, why don't you join a slimming group?'

• *Do not get impatient when the person seems to be getting worse instead of better, despite all your prayers. It can take years for an eating disorder to be overcome.*

• Write down your own daily food intake and discuss it with your own eating-disordered friend. This will help them to understand what constitutes a normal diet. (Only do this if you do not have an unhealthy attitude towards food and body weight yourself.)

• *If your husband, wife or child is anorexic/bulimic, encourage them to eat a small amount at mealtimes, then stay with them afterwards so that they are not sick.*

• Anorexia and Bulimia Care are always on the lookout for carers. If you have had experience of an eating disorder (either personally or through a relative or friend) and can devote time to pray for and talk to sufferers regularly, contact ABC at the address given in Chapter 10.

13 And Finally . . .

Stolen water is sweet, and bread eaten in secret is pleasant.

Proverbs 9.17

One o'clock. Lunch-time. At last. I switch off my computer terminal, murmur to my colleagues that I am going out to lunch, and slip on my coat. I walk briskly out of the newsroom, down the stairs and out of the building I have grown to loathe so much. I am not really going out to lunch – I ate my salad sandwiches and apple at eleven o'clock and, during the morning, supplemented them with a Twix and a few cups of hot chocolate. Now, I am going to spend the lunch-hour doing something I really do not want to do – and, at the same time, desperately need to do. I am thinking of chocolate, and I can feel the familiar sensation of something running up and down my arms; something which always happens when I am about to binge.

My first stop is the newsagent's opposite the office. I go inside and scan the sweet counter, knowing that none of the chocolate bars will satisfy my craving, yet any will suffice. I choose a Mars bar and take my place behind the woman being served. The assistant is taking a long time, and I want the Mars so much that I am tempted to run out of the shop with it. Or maybe I could eat it straight away, then pay for it, with an apologetic: 'Sorry, I was starving. I haven't eaten all day.' Increasingly agitated, I await my turn. I tear off the wrapper, and take my first bite of comforting, gooey nougat before I am out of the shop.

As I head towards the subway, I meet John, one of the

news editors. He smiles and says 'Hello'. I wish he had not seen me eating – it must be obvious to everyone that I am not happy at the newspaper and I do not want him to think I am 'comfort eating'. I walk under the subway, finishing the Mars bar, and head for the sweet kiosk at the other side. Glancing around furtively for any other newspaper colleagues, I buy a packet of Munchies.

Popping one in my mouth, I walk out of the subway and back into the not-so-fresh air. To my horror, I notice Harry; one of our reporters, coming towards me. But it is OK – he is on a late shift, just coming in, so he has not seen me eating earlier. We stop to chat. I offer him a Munchie; he accepts. We gossip for a while about the awfulness of life at the paper, which he, like me, is anxious to leave. No one is happy there it seems, but, unlike me, the other young reporters want to move on to one of the national dailies. I would hate to go to a national. The others are good reporters; I am hopeless. I am a better writer, but you do not need to write well on a newspaper. You need to be able to wring information out of people who do not wish to talk to you. I find that difficult.

After leaving Harry, I walk through the city to the main square, where I buy a Cornish pastie from Stanton's. The pastry is warm against my hands. Afterwards, I go into W. H. Smith's and flip through a couple of magazines. I find an article on bulimia nervosa. It has dawned on me recently that I must have bulimia. I used to be able to control my eating, but for the past three months have binged and purged almost daily. The binges are making me fat – this morning I weighed 7 st 10 lb, my heaviest for four years. But that was before the laxatives worked.

I need to buy more laxatives, so I go into Boots'. I really, really hate this, but I need the laxatives to maintain some control over my weight. I go up to the counter. Why do you always have to ask for the damn things, why don't they leave them out on a shelf somewhere?

Thank goodness, it is a new assistant. 'Do you sell

laxatives?' I ask, hoping that by feigning ignorance she will think they are for my grandad or somebody.

She says yes, which sort would I like? 'I think he usually has . . . is it Senokot?' I always use Senokot, I have used them for four years. Not every day like now, but fairly regularly, in an 'emergency' when I had gone over my 800-calories-a-day limit.

'Fifty or one hundred?'

I say fifty in case she suspects they are for me. Stupid, really. I will only have to go through the whole rigmarole again in a few days' time.

I resist the urge to buy a bar of chocolate from Boots', because that really would be giving the game away. I buy a Cadbury's Dairy Milk from a kiosk and glance at my watch. Twenty to two. I am at work till six today. What will the afternoon hold? I pray that I will be able to cope with whatever it is and that the time will pass quickly.

Before returning to the office, I consume a tuna sandwich and an iced bun. Then I enter the newsroom, clutching a can of Diet Coke. 'You'll get fat on that,' jokes Marion, one of the reporters, a hefty woman who chain-smokes all day long. I laugh, but I know I am going to be huge if I carry on eating like this.

John, the news editor, asks me to do a load of picture captions. I take the photographs and contact lists and start ringing people up for information. Picture captions are mundane, but at least they are safe. I can handle picture captions – but not hassling bereaved relatives, or trying to squeeze information from unhelpful police officers.

I could do the captions in an hour, but I spin them out for the entire afternoon, afraid that once I have finished, I will be given something awful to do – or, even worse, something that might involve working past six o'clock. At four-thirty, Nick, the chief sports sub-editor arrives, and I send him a greeting on the computer system. Instantly, a reply flashes up on my screen. The time goes faster as we type messages back and forth. He has asked me out a couple of times, but

I had the excuse that I was seeing someone else. Nick does not know that Tom and I split up about five weeks ago, and I hope he does not find out. I do not want a relationship, not while I am like this. It is horrible being touched when you are fat.

At last six o'clock crawls round and I can go home. I eat some Rolos on the way back. I have been living with my parents since leaving university and finding a job on a local daily paper, and my mother will have a healthy low-calorie meal ready for me when I return. She thinks I am still dieting, and does not know about my binges.

Tonight, she has prepared fish and salad. 'I bet you're hungry, aren't you?' she asks. 'Not especially,' I reply, going upstairs to change. My skirt is tight after all the bingeing, so I put on track-suit pants and a baggy T-shirt. I eat the fish and salad, not enjoying it, because I feel so full and fat. Afterwards, I take the dog for a walk, and spend the evening in my room, reading. Since Tom and I parted, I have no social life at all.

At ten o'clock I swallow a handful of laxatives, because I need them to work before I leave the house at seven-thirty tomorrow. I undress, pinching my bloated stomach and chubby thighs, hating myself for being so horribly fat. Tomorrow, I decide, I will skip breakfast and take no money to work. I will just eat a sandwich and an apple and whatever we have for tea. If I do not go on a strict diet soon, I shall be even more enormous than I am already.

The next day is Tuesday, the day I compile a weekly equestrian column for the sports pages. I like working on the column – it keeps me busy, but not under pressure.

The laxatives work before I go out, and I arrive at the paper feeling light and small. I have no money, so I know I am safe from bingeing today. It is a relief. Mike, today's news editor, sends me to coroner's court to cover two full inquests and three opening inquests. I like covering inquests – the coroner's office always provides names and addresses of both deceased and witnesses so you do not have to hassle anybody. The only problem is that the coroner always carries on straight through lunch-time, which is a problem for a food addict like me.

I sit through the inquests, then phone them over to the paper. The afternoon is spent compiling the equestrian column. I ring Nick Skelton to ask about a new horse he is riding at a local show. As I write my copy, I wonder why someone with a job envied by thousands of would-be journalists should be so unhappy as to eat and take laxatives all the time.

I feel happy about my day and return home, feeling hungry. My stomach is rumbling, which pleases me – I must have burnt off all the calories I consumed yesterday. Tonight I enjoy my meal. I take the dog for a walk, then go upstairs to read. My parents always go out on Tuesday evenings and as the time inches towards nine o'clock, I start to think about peanut-butter sandwiches and can feel something running up and down my arms. I feel excited about being in the house alone free to eat – and apprehensive about whether I can control the amount I consume. I grow increasingly uptight until my parents have left the house.

I go into the kitchen and make myself a peanut-butter sandwich. I do not switch on the light, in case the neighbours or a passer-by notices me preparing and eating food. I eat the sandwich and want more. I eat some cream crackers, some digestive biscuits, peanut butter straight from the jar. I am always careful to ensure my mother will not notice anything has been taken. I take a sausage roll from the freezer, and put it in the oven. It takes twenty minutes to heat up, an eternity. To pass the time, I eat icing sugar straight from the packet; handfuls of sultanas; more peanut butter; two more crackers, this time spread with jam; some of the dog's Good Boy chocolates. At last the sausage roll is ready. I do not enjoy it. I feel bloated and have a headache – the beginning of a 'binge hangover'. I wash up the plate and cutlery I have used, feeling depressed. I shed a few tears thinking about how much weight I must have put on after being so good all day. Then I take a can of Diet Coke from the fridge and use it to swill down the laxatives.

—

I go to bed when my parents return. I feel tense when my mother goes into the kitchen – will she notice any food missing? She does not. I lie in bed and pray that God will help me overcome this constant, frightening desire to binge. A small part of me believes he will. But the rest wonders if it will ever stop.

But it did. And that is partly why I have ended up writing this book.

That was me ten years ago. I was a shy 23-year-old trainee journalist struggling to survive in the tough profession I had wanted to work in since my early teens. My sense of inadequacy, my fear of admitting to others that I could not, after all, cope with my 'dream job' and my uncertainty about possible, alternative careers, combined to 'make' me turn to food.

Today, it is hard to relate to those binges. I now have a hearty appetite, I eat when I am hungry and stop when I am full. I no longer worry about my weight because I know how much food my body needs to be healthy. I am one of the fortunate ones. As the stories in this book show, it could all have ended so differently.

It was a long struggle to stop bingeing. The purging stopped first, then (after several years) the bingeing, and finally the desire to be thin ebbed away. I cannot pinpoint when each stage occurred, because the process was gradual. Along the way, though, came many tears, many prayers, many failed attempts to diet, some changes of attitude, some changes of lifestyle.

Now, in retrospect, I sometimes think: If *only* I had sought help for my eating disorder when I was twenty-three. If *only* I had admitted that I had chosen the wrong profession and got out then instead of forcing myself to carry on. If *only* I had sought counselling for my deep sense of inadequacy instead of thinking success in my career would make me feel good about myself. But it is no use thinking like that. And, in a sense, maybe facing different issues at different stages of my life has been better than trying to tackle everything at once.

I hope, though, that anyone who reads this book and recognizes that they have a problem with food and body image *will* seek help and support – straight away. It is not easy changing your attitude to food and weight or admitting you have a problem but, in the years to come when you're free of all those hang-ups, it surely is worth it.

Notes

Chapter 1

1 Andrew Morton, *Diana, Her True Story* (O'Mara Books, 1992).

Chapter 3

1 It is interesting that a gallstone operation should have spawned one of the top selling diet manuals, since some medics have claimed that gallstones can be caused by too rigid dieting. (This was among the anti-diet arguments put forward in Alice Mahon's private member's bill.) Rosemary Conley had dieted prior to discovering and publishing her *Hip and Thigh Diet* and had also run her own slimming clubs, but whether her own gallstone problems were a result of rigid dieting is not known.
2 Ramona Koval, *Eating Your Heart Out: Food, Shape and the Diet Industry* (Penguin 1989).

Chapter 4

1 *Chicago Sun-Times* (24 July 1972).
2 Ray Coleman, *The Carpenters: The Untold Story* (Boxtree, 1995).
3 Rosemary Conley interviewed by Pete Jay, Spring Harvest, 1992.

Chapter 5

1 *Daily Mail* (28 September 1994).
2 Koval, *Eating Your Heart Out.*
3 Jo Ind, *Fat Is a Spiritual Issue* (Mowbray, 1993).
4 *People* magazine (February 1992).
5 Marie Chapian and Neva Coyle, *Free To Be Slim* (Kingsway, 1985).

Chapter 6

1 Ind, *Fat Is a Spiritual Issue.*
2 Susie Orbach, *Fat Is a Feminist Issue* (Arrow, 1978).
3 Naomi Wolf, *The Beauty Myth* (Vintage, 1991).
4 Paulette Maisner, *Feasting and Fasting* (Fontana, 1985).

Chapter 7

1 Anthony Campolo, *Seven Deadly Sins* (Victor Books, 1987).
2 Ind, *Fat Is a Spiritual Issue.*
3 Rosemary Conley, speaking at Spring Harvest, 1992.
4 Jill Welbourne interviewed in *Woman Alive* (July 1993).
5 Ronald Rolheiser, *The Shattered Lantern: Rediscovering the Felt Presence of God* (Hodder & Stoughton, 1994).

Chapter 8

1 Mary Evans Young, interviewed by Judi Spiers, Radio Two (4 February 1995).
2 Rolheiser, *The Shattered Lantern.*
3 Ind, *Fat Is a Spiritual Issue.*

Chapter 9

1 Rolheiser, *The Shattered Lantern.*

Chapter 11

1 Campolo, *Seven Deadly Sins.*
2 Ind, *Fat Is a Spiritual Issue.*
3 Selwyn Hughes, *God Wants You Whole* (Kingsway, 1984).